SHAKESPEARE IN LOVE

Shakespeare in Love

adapted for the stage by
Lee Hall

based on the screenplay by
Marc Norman & Tom Stoppard

Grove Press
New York

Published simultaneously in Canada
Printed in the United States of America

First published in 2014 by Faber and Faber Limited
74–77 Great Russell Street, London WC1B 3DA

ISBN 978-0-8021-2395-4
eISBN 978-0-8021-9106-9

Grove Press
an imprint of Grove Atlantic
154 West 14th Street
New York, NY 10011

Distributed by Publishers Group West

groveatlantic.com

15 16 17 18   10 9 8 7 6 5 4 3 2 1

Shakespeare in Love was first presented at the Noël Coward Theatre, London, produced by Disney Theatrical Productions and Sonia Friedman Productions, on 22 July 2014. The cast, in alphabetical order, was as follows:

Tilney Ian Bartholomew
Will Shakespeare Tom Bateman
Ralph Tony Bell
Kate Daisy Boulton
Viola de Lesseps Lucy Briggs-Owen
Queen Elizabeth Anna Carteret
Ensemble Michael Chadwick
Henslowe Paul Chahidi
Ensemble Tom Clegg
Ensemble Ryan Donaldson
Robin / Frees / Musical Director Tim van Eyken
Molly / Mistress Quickly Janet Fullerlove
Burbage David Ganly
Sir Robert de Lesseps Richard Howard
Sam / Fight Captain / Assistant Dance Captain Harry Jardine
Ensemble Amy Marchant
Nurse Abigail McKern
Peter / Barman / Dance Captain Sandy Murray
Marlowe David Oakes
Wabash Patrick Osborne
Ensemble Timothy O'Hara
Adam / Boatman / Musician Thomas Padden
Wessex Alistair Petrie
Ned Alleyn Doug Rao
Lambert / Guard / Musician Elliott Rennie

Fennyman Ferdy Roberts
Webster Colin Ryan
Nol / Musician Charlie Tighe

Director Declan Donnellan
Designer Nick Ormerod
Music Paddy Cunneen
Choreography Jane Gibson
Lighting Neil Austin
Sound Simon Baker
Associate Director Oli Rose
Casting Siobhan Bracke CDG
Fight Director Terry King

Characters

Ned Alleyn
Boatman
Molly
Kate
Musicians, Attendants

SHAKESPEARE IN LOVE

Act One

Will Shall I compare the.

The . . .

The company create Will's desk. They assemble around the desk and Will takes his place. Throughout the play, wherever possible, the company observe the action when they are not part of it.

Shall I compare . . . thee? Shall I compare thee! . . . to a . . . to a . . .?

Shall I compare thee to a . . . sum . . . a sum . . . a something, something . . .

Damn it.

Shall I compare thee to a mummer's play?

Shall I compare thee . . . to . . . an autumn morning? An afternoon in springtime? Zounds.

This is not right either. Marlowe appears from within the ensemble and the two move freely around the ensemble.

Marlowe A sonnet. I thought you were writing a play.

Will A month overdue to Henslowe but nothing comes. I have lost my gift, Kit. I don't know what it is. My quill is broken, my well is dry. The proud tower of the imagination hath collapsed completely.

Marlowe Interesting. And how are your marital relations?

Will The Ardens?

3

Marlowe The bedroom.

Will As cold as her heart.

Marlowe So you are free to love.

Will Yet not to write, so it seems. Leave me, Kit.

Marlowe I've almost finished my new play for Burbage. More blood and thunder but he pays well for it. I hear he plays your *Two Gentlemen of Verona* for Her Majesty this very afternoon.

Will My play, for the Queen!

Marlowe A summer's day.

Will What?

Marlowe 'A summer's day'. Start with something lovely, temperate and thoroughly trite. Gives you somewhere to go.

Marlowe leaves. The ensemble reconvene around Will's desk.

Will (*unconvinced*) A summer's day?!

He writes reluctantly.

Shall I compare thee . . . to a . . . summer's day? Mmm?

Thou art more . . . something something something . . .

SCENE TWO
HANGING OF HENSLOWE

Henslowe Arrrrgghhh!!

As Henslowe screams the ensemble scatter, many of them remaining onstage, observing. Henslowe is strung up over hot coals. Lambert holds a rope to move him up and down.

Fennyman You mongrel! Why do you howl when it is I who am bitten? What am I, Mr Lambert?

Lambert Bitten, Mr Fennyman.

Fennyman How badly, Mr Frees?

Frees Twelve pounds, one shilling and fourpence, Mr Fennyman, plus interest.

Henslowe Aaarrggh. I can pay you!

Fennyman When? Mr Henslowe?

Henslowe Two weeks. Three at the most. Aaarrgh. For pity's sake.

Fennyman Drop him. Where will you get . . .

Frees Sixteen pounds, five shillings and ninepence . . .

Henslowe I have a wonderful new play!

Fennyman A play?

Henslowe A play, Mr Fennyman.

Fennyman Let him have it.

Henslowe It's a comedy.

Fennyman Cut off his nose.

Henslowe A new comedy.

Fennyman And his ear.

Henslowe By Will Shakespeare.

Fennyman Who?

Henslowe Richard Burbage and his men play his *Two Gentlemen of Verona* today for the Queen at Whitehall.

Fennyman Shakespeare? Never heard of him.

Henslowe I think he has potential. We will be partners, Mr Fennyman.

Fennyman Partners?

Henslowe The play's a crowd-tickler – mistaken identities, a shipwreck, a pirate king, a bit with a dog and love triumphant.

Frees Didn't you see that one, Lambert?

Lambert Yeah, and I didn't like it.

Henslowe But this time it is by Shakespeare.

Fennyman What's it called?

Henslowe *Romeo and Ethel the Pirate's Daughter.*

Fennyman Good title.

Henslowe is released.

A play, that takes time. Find actors . . . rehearsals, let's say open in three weeks. That's – what – five hundred groundlings at tuppence each, in addition four hundred backsides at threepence – a penny extra for a cushion, call it two hundred cushions, say two performances for safety. How much is that, Mr Frees?

Frees Twenty pounds to the penny.

Fennyman Correct!

Henslowe But I have to pay the actors and the author.

Fennyman A share of the profits.

Henslowe There's never any.

Fennyman Of course not!

Henslowe Mr Fennyman, I think you may have hit on something.

From within the watching ensemble Burbage comes.

Burbage Gentlemen of Verona.

Fennyman Sign here.

Burbage This is your two-minute call.

Henslowe It's blank.

Fennyman I know.

Fennyman, Frees, Lambert and Henslowe take their leave as the new scene begins.

SCENE THREE
TWO GENTLEMEN OF VERONA

We are backstage at Whitehall Palace.

Burbage Act One, Scene One. Wardrobe Mistress, quickly.

Mistress Quickly Ready, sir!

Burbage Maestro.

Maestro Ready.

Burbage And silence.

Will Burbage!

Burbage Oh God, an author.

Will How dare you perform me here in front of the Queen without my say-so? I am still owed half of the commission.

Burbage Not from me. I stole it from Henslowe. If he stole it from you that's his business.

Will Why is there a dog?

Burbage The Queen loves a dog.

Will There's no dog in my *Two Gentlemen of Verona*.

Burbage There is now.

Will I demand to be paid for this, Burbage.

Burbage I told you I will make you a partner, Shakespeare. For fifty pounds. Your hireling days will be over.

Will Where will I go for fifty pounds?

Burbage I hear Anne Hathaway is a woman of property.

Will No, she has a cottage. What would you give me for a comedy all but done?

Burbage What's the part?

Will Romeo. Wit, swordsman, lover.

Burbage And the title?

Will *Romeo*.

Burbage I shall play him. Here's two sovereigns, and two more when you show me the pages. Now *begone*!

Tilney My masters, are you mad? Her Majesty is waiting!

Burbage We are ready, Mr Tilney.

Tilney Is that the dog?

Burbage Yes.

Tilney But it's a different dog.

Burbage The other was eaten by a bear.

Tilney The only reason the Queen asked to see this circus – was the dog.

Actor But Spot can do tricks, sir, look. Spot, jump!

Burbage I assure you he brings the house down at the Curtain.

Tilney It doesn't look funny.

Burbage Nerves. He's never played the Palace.

Tilney If you don't go up this instant I will revoke your charter.

Company One, two, three . . . To silence.

Music. Curtains open to reveal Queen and Court. Tilney coughs.

Queen Is this the one with the dog?

Tilney Yes, your Majesty. *The Two Gentlemen of Verona,* an Italianate romance on the nature of love, with a dog.

Queen Excellent. I very much liked the dog.

Actor
Cease to persuade, my loving Proteus.
Home-keeping youth have ever homely wits.

Continues in dumbshow.

Henslowe I thought you'd be here. Where is my play? Shakespeare.

Will All locked safe in here.

Henslowe Locked? I gave you three sovereigns a month ago.

Will Half what you owed me. I am still owed for one *Gentleman of Verona.*

Henslowe What is money to you and me? I am without a single new play while Burbage is invited here to Court and receives ten pounds to play your piece written for *my* theatre at *my* risk.

Will Mr Henslowe, will you lend me fifty pounds?

Henslowe What for?

Will Burbage offers me a partnership in the Chamberlain's Men.

Henslowe Cut out my heart – feed my liver to the dogs!

Will I'll take that as a no, then.

Henslowe I'm a dead man and buggered to boot. I hear Burbage has a brand new Christopher Marlowe for the Curtain and I have nothing for the Rose. When will I get it, Will?

Will As soon as I have found my muse.

Henslowe Who is it this time?

Will It is always Aphrodite.

Henslowe Aphrodite Baggott who does it behind the Dog and Biscuit?

Actor
What light is light if Silvia be not seen?
What joy is joy if Silvia be not by?

Dog enters and jumps on the actor speaking. Burbage in the wings motions for the other actor to help.

Unless it be to think that she is by
And feed –

The dog is causing problems.

– upon the shadow of perfection.

Burbage Spot! Spot! Out, damn Spot!

He finally removes the dog.

Henslowe See. Comedy. That's what they want. Love and a bit with a dog.

The action continues but the lights and sound fade on the stage and the auditorium. We focus on Will's chagrin.

Will I refuse to watch this shambles.

Will has had enough – he slopes off. Henslowe is intently watching the audience's reaction to the play.

Henslowe Where are you going?

Will To hang myself. Ask for me tomorrow and you shall find me in a grave pit.

Henslowe Wait. There is a lady who knows your play by heart. Look how she mouths the words.

Henslowe turns to show Will the appreciative audience member.

Will – Will . . .?

Will has gone. The onstage music that lay under the Two Gentlemen of Verona *scene moves into an introduction to Viola's room.*

SCENE FOUR
VIOLA'S FIRST BEDROOM

As the scene changes Viola steps out of the tableau of the 'onstage' auditorium and walks downstage, delivering the speech from Two Gentlemen *as the new scene sets around her. She plays to various members of the company, who watch appreciatively.*

Viola

> What light is light if Silvia be not seen
> What joy is joy if Silvia be not by?
> Unless it be to think that she is by and feed
> Upon the shadow of perfection.

SONG – 'O MISTRESS MINE'

> *O mistress mine, where are you roaming*
> *O stay and hear your true love's coming*
> *That can sing both high and low.*

Viola

> Except I be by Silvia in the night,
> There is no music in the nightingale,
> Unless I look on Silvia in the day,
> There is no day for me to look upon.

The watchers applaud.

Such poetry . . .

The watchers disappear; reality reasserting itself.

But how can one care for Silvia while she is – by the order of the Lord Chamberlain – played by a pipsqueak boy in petticoats!

Nurse I liked the dog.

Viola Stage love will never be real love until we women can be on stage ourselves. Yet when can we see another?

Nurse When the Queen commands it.

Viola But at the playhouse.

Nurse Playhouses are not for well-born ladies.

Viola I am not so well-born.

Nurse Well-monied is the same as well-born and well-married better than both. Lord Wessex was looking at you tonight.

Viola All the men at Court are without poetry. If they look at me they see my father's fortune. I will have poetry in my life. And adventure. And love. Love above all.

Nurse Like Valentine and Silvia?

Viola No – not the artful postures of love, but the love that overthrows life. Unbiddable, ungovernable, like a riot in the heart, and nothing to be done, come ruin or rapture. Love like there has never been in a play. I will have love or I will end my days –

Nurse As a nurse?

Viola But I would be Valentine and Silvia too somehow. Good Nurse, God save you and goodnight. I would stay asleep my whole life if I could dream myself into a company of players.

Suddenly waiters are on shouting orders to the kitchen. The musicians play tavern music.

Musician Calves' head with oysters and the coxcomb tartlet, table nine.

SCENE FIVE
THE TAVERN

We find ourselves in a tavern.

Ralph Ah Mr Henslowe. How goes it, sir?

Henslowe Very well. Very well, Ralph, my good man. Some food and drink.

Ralph Well, the special today is a pig's foot marinated in juniper berry vinegar served with a buckwheat pancake and a burdock salad.

Henslowe I'll have a pie and pint. And have one for yourself, Master Ralph.

As Ralph goes off to fetch the order, Henslowe is pushed on to a table and stretched either side by two henchmen who have arrived with Fennyman.

Fennyman Next time we take your boots off. Stretch him!

Henslowe Mr Fennyman. What have I done?

Fennyman That is the question. Nothing. (*Turning to the Musicians.*) Shut it! (*To Henslowe.*) Why haven't you started.

Henslowe Oh, it's all taken care of, gentlemen. It all takes time.

Fennyman Where is the manuscript, Mr Henslowe?

Henslowe A manuscript. Let me explain about the theatre business. The natural condition is one of insurmountable obstacles on the road to imminent disaster. One must never expect a manuscript at this stage. That is an impediment to look forward to. But it always works out in the end.

Fennyman How?

Henslowe I don't know. It's a mystery.

Fennyman No *Pirates*, you're a dead man. Come on.

Fennyman and his men leave. Henslowe knocks back the drink and sits at a table. A waiter arrives.

Ralph Did I hear you have a play, Mr Henslowe?

Shakespeare enters and, avoiding Henslowe, makes his way to the bar.

Henslowe Shakespeare is writing as we speak.

Ralph Is there anything for me?

Henslowe You're a perfect Pirate King, Ralph, but I hear you are a drunken sot.

Ralph Never when I'm working.

Nol A play, Mr Henslowe?

Henslowe And there's a nice little part for you, Master Nol.

Nol Thank you very much.

Ralph What about the money?

Henslowe It won't cost you a penny. We will all share the profits. Auditions this afternoon.

Will Auditions? Where are your usual men?

Henslowe With Ned Alleyn in the provinces. God knows when they will return. We cannot delay. We need bodies, Will.

Will But not these pickled hams.

Henslowe Auditions round the back in five minutes. If you are not there, Will, I will cast it myself. Ralph, bring the pie round.

Nol Mr Henslowe!

Henslowe leaves with Nol in tow. Will goes to the bar.

Will Give me to drink mandragora.

Barman Straight up?

Marlowe Bring my friend a beaker of your best brandy. How goes it, Will?

Will Wonderful, wonderful. Most wonderful.

Marlowe Burbage says you're also writing him a play!

Will I have the chinks to show for it.

He puts a coin down for the drinks.

I insist, and a beaker for Mr Marlowe. And how is yours?

Marlowe Just finished. My best since *Faustus*.

Will I love your early work. This time?

Marlowe *The Massacre at Paris*. And yours?

Will *Romeo and Ethel the Pirate's Daughter*. Yes, I know.

Marlowe What's the story?

Will Well, there's this pirate . . . In truth I haven't written a word.

Marlowe Well, Romeo is . . . Italian.

Will Marvellous.

Marlowe Always in and out of love.

Will That's good. Until he meets . . .

Marlowe Ethel.

Will Really?

Suddenly Marlowe comes up with something.

Marlowe Juliet.

Will Juliet?

Marlowe The daughter of his enemy.

Will The daughter of his enemy.

Marlowe His best friend is killed in a duel by Juliet's brother or something. His name is Mercutio.

Will Mercutio. Good name.

Will What happens to Ethel?

Marlowe (*deliberately preposterous*) Marries a blackamoor and is strangled with a handkerchief.

Will (*sarcastically*) Inspired. Thank you, Kit.

Nol Will. Mr Henslowe is about to start the auditions for *Romeo*.

Marlowe I thought the play was for Burbage?

Will That's a different one.

Marlowe A different one you haven't written?

Will Next!

SCENE SIX
AUDITIONS

Will Thank you, and now for your modern piece.

Robin
Was this the face that launched a thousand ships
And burnt the topless towers of Ilium?
Sweet Helen, make me immortal with a kiss.

Will Thank you. Next!

Henslowe We have to cast somebody.

Will Next!

Adam I would like to give you something from *Faustus* by Christopher Marlowe.

Will How refreshing.

Adam
Was this the face that launched a thousand ships . . .

Will Next!

John Webster comes in. Will takes one look and dismisses him.

Next.

Webster But I haven't started.

Will No doubt you will be giving us your Christopher Marlowe?

Webster Yes.

Will 'The topless towers of Ilium'?

Webster ~~Tamburlaine the Great~~.

Will Tamburlaine the Great was a bloodthirsty tyrant. Not a ten-year-old malkin from Cheapside.

Henslowe Maybe he could be Ethel.

Will This is absurd.

Webster (*plays Tamburlaine with vicious gusto*)
    Go, villain, cast thee headlong from a rock,
    Or rip thy bowels, and rend out thy heart,
    T'appease my wrath; or else I'll torture thee,
    Searing thy hateful flesh with burning irons . . .

Will Thank you!

Webster
    And drops of scalding lead, while all thy joints
    Be rack'd and beat asunder with the wheel.

Will Enough!

Webster I can do Barabas. Or the gory bit from the *Agamemnon*.

Will We've seen enough.

John Webster goes.

Henslowe I liked him.

Will Next.

Henslowe Ah, Mr Wabash!

Wabash W-w-w-was th-th-this the f-f-face . . .

Henslowe Very good, Mr Wabash. Excellent. Report to the property master.

Wabash Th-th-th-thank you very m-m-m-much.

Henslowe My tailor. Wants to be an actor. I have a few debts here and there. Well, that seems to be everybody. Did you see a Romeo?

Will I did not.

Henslowe Well, to my work, and you to yours. When can I see pages?

Will Tomorrow.

Henslowe Tomorrow and . . .

Will Tomorrow.

Henslowe leaves.

Viola/Kent May I begin, sir?

Will Your name?

Viola/Kent Thomas Kent. I would like to do a speech by a writer who commands the heart of every player, sir.

Will Yes, I am sure.

Will sits up.

Viola/Kent
What light is light if Silvia be not seen,
What joy is joy if Silvia be not by?
Unless it be to think that she is by
And feed upon the shadow of perfection
Except I be by Silvia in the night
There is no music in the nightingale,
Unless I look on Silvia in the day
There is no day for me to look upon.

Will Where did you learn to do that?

Viola/Kent At the playhouse, sir.

Will There is no playhouse in London where my verse is spoke truly.

Viola/Kent Are you Mr Shakespeare?

Will I have not seen you audition before, Mr Kent.

Viola/Kent I am new to London, sir. I am from the country staying at the de Lesseps. In Cheam.

Will Please, sir. Speak some more. Without your hat.

Viola/Kent My hat?

Will Let me see your face.

Will comes over to Kent.

Viola/Kent No!

Will Please. Speak it to me again. Let it trip off the tongue.

Will tries to take Kent's hat.

Viola/Kent Sir!

Will It's a love scene. Please take off your hat.

She continues to evade him.

Viola/Kent Give me my hat, sir.

Marlowe comes in and Viola runs straight into him.

Marlowe Any luck?

Marlowe likes what he sees. They dance around each other before Viola escapes and leaves

Who was he?

Will My Romeo. Hands off.

The scene changes to De Lesseps Hall. Music. Kent/Viola runs on to the waiting Nurse, while around them the ball begins to take shape.

Nurse My Lady. Where have you been?

Viola I have been to audition for the theatre.

Nurse I'll be in my grave if they find out. Quick indoors, you must get ready for the ball. The guests are already arriving. Special guests too as well you should know. Your father is waiting to introduce you to Lord Wessex. You'll drive me to madness.

As Viola and Nurse exit the stage bursts with music and life.

SCENE SEVEN
THE BALLROOM

The stage is strung with nightlights for the alfresco ball. Out of the action emerges a conversation . . .

Wessex Where is she, Sir Robert? I am starting to wonder if she is a mythical beast of your invention.

Sir Robert de Lesseps She will come, I assure you. She is a beauty, my lord, as would take a king to church for a dowry of nutmeg.

Wessex My plantations in Virginia are not mortgaged for a nutmeg. I have an ancient name that will bring you preferment when your grandson is a Wessex. Is she fertile?

Sir Robert de Lesseps She will breed. If she do not, send her back.

Wessex And obedient?

Sir Robert de Lesseps As any mule in Christendom. But if you are the man to ride her, there are rubies in the saddle.

Wessex I like her.

Sir Robert de Lesseps Come, she will be down any moment.

At the gate to the garden Will appears with Marlowe.

Guard Sorry. Can't come in without an invite. This is a proper ball. For civilised people.

Will We are civilised people. I'm an actor and this is Christopher Marlowe, one of Europe's leading writers.

Marlowe Hello.

Guard I don't care if you're Beaumont and Fletcher. You're not getting in without an invite.

Will But I have a letter. For Thomas Kent.

The Nurse, who happens to be near the gate, pushes past.

Nurse Who asks for Thomas Kent?

Will Will Shakespeare, actor, poet and playwright of the Rose. Master Kent auditioned for me this afternoon.

Nurse Master Kent?

Will You know him?

Nurse Yes. He is my . . . nephew.

Will I have a letter. To offer him the lead part in my play.

Nurse I will see he gets it, sirs. Catling, let them through.

They are reluctantly let in.

PAVANE DANCE – 'WHAT IS LOVE?'

Company
> *What is love?*
> *Is love hereafter?*
> *Present mirth is present laughter.*
> *What's to come is still unsure*
> *Youth's a stuff will not endure.*

Sir Robert de Lesseps My daughter.

Wessex Yes. I think she will do. She will do very nicely.

Will By all the stars in heaven, who is she?

Nurse That's My Lady Viola de Lesseps.

Marlowe Dream on, Will Shakespeare.

Will O she doth teach the torches to burn bright.

Marlowe Forget it!

Will I will speak to her.

Marlowe We will be run out of here.

Will It is a free country, is it not?

Marlowe Have a drink, Will!

> *Silence.*
> *Sir Robert takes Viola's hand and delivers her to*
> *Wessex for the dance. Will stops in horror.*

Sir Robert de Lesseps Viola, My Lord Wessex.

Wessex Enchanted.

> *Music continues. Dance changes to cascada.*
> *Will is thwarted. A flurry of excitement. Dancers*
> *take the stage, obscuring Will. All in time to the music.*

Wessex My Lady Viola.

Viola My Lord.

Wessex I have spoken to your father.

Viola So, My Lord. I speak with him every day.

Wessex I have spoken to your father about your future.

Viola I trust you found it of interest. I rarely know what is going to happen next.

> *Wessex and Viola are parted and suddenly she is*
> *partnered with Shakespeare.*

Viola Good sir!

Will My lady.

Viola Are you not the poet William Shakespeare?

Will I am not, my lady.

Viola But sir, I have seen you at the playhouse.

Will I am a poet no longer. As I have seen a beauty that would prove all my poetry prose.

Viola What brings you to my house?

Will I came to seek one who would make my words as fluent as the river. Now I find one who makes me dumb.

The dance changes again and Wessex and Viola are face to face.

Wessex I need a dowry, your family seek a title. It seems our fortunes are well met.

Viola You think only of 'a fortune', My Lord. Fate pays no heed to worldly commerce.

Wessex You mistake the times, finance and futures are inextricably linked.

Will This is a dream.

Viola Dreams are the children of an idle brain, begot of nothing but vain fantasy which is as thin of substance as the air.

Will Did you really just say that?

Viola Indeed I truly hope, sir, this is no dream.

Will If we are awake let me dream you such words that will make you immortal.

Viola Good sir. None can be immortal. I only dream of being alive.

Will Then I will be your poet.

Will breaks the pattern of the dance and Wessex has overheard him.

Wessex Poet? Nay, you are a knave, sir.

Wessex threatens him briefly and they continue to the dance, this time Will and Wessex dancing near one another.

Will How do I offend, My Lord?

Wessex By coveting my property. I cannot shed blood in her house but I will cut your throat anon. You have a name?

Will Christopher Marlowe at your service.

Wessex rejoins the dance, taking Viola for a partner. He smiles. She is not happy.

Viola You smile, sir. Is there anything wrong?

Wessex Not any more.

They dance. The song comes to an end. They curtsy to each other. The scene breaks as Viola turns to the Nurse.

Nurse Look, My Lady, a letter to Thomas Kent.

Viola Who from?

Nurse From the playwright, William Shakespeare.

Music. The stage transforms. The trappings of the ball disappear and we are in the garden below Viola's balcony. Will and Marlowe sit gazing at the stars, with the Nurse and Viola above.

THE BALCONY SCENE

Nurse He was desperate to speak to 'Master Kent'.

Viola Oh. I can't believe it.

She reads the letter.

'I have never heard my words spoken with such honesty. I am writing a comedy of quarrelling families reconciled in the discovery of Romeo to be the very same Capulet cousin stolen from the cradle and fostered to manhood by his Montague mother that was robbed of her own child by the Pirate King! And I would have you play Romeo Montague, a young gentleman of Verona.'

Nurse Verona, again?!

Viola Is Master Shakespeare not handsome?

Nurse He looks well enough for a mountebank.

Viola Oh, Nurse! He would give Thomas Kent the life of Viola de Lesseps' dreaming.

Nurse My Lady, this play will end badly.

Viola 'Tis a comedy. It ends with a pirate jig. As you love me and as I love you, you will bind my breast and buy me a boy's wig. Rehearsals start tomorrow.

Nurse Your father?

Viola From tomorrow away in the country for three weeks.

Will and Marlowe have noticed the pair above.

Marlowe (*sotto voce*) Look. There she is.

Will Shh.

Marlowe Go on and talk to her.

Will You'll have us caught.

Marlowe Under the balcony.

Marlowe and Will conceal themselves, waiting for the Nurse to leave Viola alone.

Marlowe Just give her a whistle.

Will The nurse is there.

Nurse My Lady. You'll catch your death out here.

Viola Leave me, Nursey.

Nurse Believe me this will all end in tears.

Exit Nurse. Viola reads the letter again.

Marlowe Look, she has your letter.

Viola Romeo, Romeo . . . a young gentleman of Verona. A comedy. By William Shakespeare.

Marlowe Well, go on.

Will My Lady.

Viola Who is there?

Will Will Shakespeare.

Nurse (*off*) Madam!

Viola Anon, good Nurse, anon. Master Shakespeare?

Will The same, alas.

Viola Why alas?

Will A lowly player.

Viola Alas indeed, for I thought you the highest poet of my esteem and a writer of the most brilliant comedies that capture my heart.

Will Oh, I am him too.

Nurse (*off*) Lady Viola.

Viola Anon. Anon. (*To Will.*) I will come again.

She goes in to deal with the Nurse.

Marlowe Enough. The trap is laid, she takes the bait.

Will Nonsense. I'm just getting somewhere.

Marlowe 'A lowly player'?! Get out before the whole thing is ruined.

Viola returns.

Viola If they find you here they will kill you.

Will And you can bring them with a word.

Viola Not for the world! Yours are the only words mine ears can bear to hear. Speak to me. Inspire me.

Will (*trying rather pathetically to be poetic*) Alas I cannot for I am . . . struck dumb by your beauty.

Viola Come, come. Good poet. These are hackneyed tropes. Extemporise, improvise. Fill me with your words.

Marlowe Leave.

Viola is waiting, expectantly.

Will (*to Viola*) Now?

Viola Yes. Translate our base tongue into the golden verse of love.

Will Erm . . . (*Under his breath.*) *Pigs!*

Viola What was that?

Marlowe Recite something you know.

Will I've gone blank.

Marlowe Anything.

Will Erm . . . erm . . . Help me, Kit!

Marlowe 'Shall I compare thee . . . ?'

Relieved by this prompt, he recites with confidence.

Will
Shall I compare thee to a summer's day?
Thou art more lovely and more temperate.

He looks to Marlowe for appreciation for the completed line.

Marlowe It's not Philip Sidney.

Viola Go on.

Will (*to Marlowe*) That's as far as I got.

Marlowe As far as you got?!

Will Help me, Kit!

Viola More, my love.

Panic down below, so Marlowe improvises, prompting Will from below the balcony.

Marlowe
Rough winds do shake . . .

Will
Rough winds do shake . . .

Marlowe
The darling buds of . . . May

Will Isn't that spring?

Marlowe It rhymes with 'day'.

And summer's lease hath . . .

Will
And summer's lease hath . . .

Marlowe
All too short a date.

Will (*to Marlowe*)
All too short a date.

Viola Oh, this is beautiful, Will . . . More . . .

Marlowe Dum di dum di dum di . . . got it . . .

But thy eternal summer shall not fade –

Will (*repeating as he goes*)
But thy eternal summer shall not fade
Nor lose possession of that fair thou owest.

Marlowe
Nor shall death . . .

Will Don't mention death . . .

Marlowe Death is good.

Nor shall death brag thou wander'st in his shade.

Will
Nor shall death brag thou wandrest in his shade.

Marlowe
When in eternal lines to time thou growest.

Will (*to Marlowe*) What does that mean?

Marlowe Just say it.
Will
When in eternal lines to time thou growest . . .

Marlowe
So long as men can breathe . . .
Will
So long as men can breathe – (*adding his own bit*)
or eyes can see . . .

30

Marlowe Very good . . .

Will (*now inspired*)
  So long lives this –

Marlowe That's it.

Will
  – and this gives life to thee.

Marlowe Bravo.

Will I have it back, Kit.

Viola Oh, it's beautiful.

Will It's nothing.

Viola Only you could have conceived such a thing.

Will I think it lacks something in the middle.

Viola Not another word. It's perfect.

Nurse (*off*) Madam.

Viola I must go.

Will No. But I am a poor poet. I have not had payment.

Viola Such sublime eloquence is God's own recompense.

Will (*very pleased with himself*) Yet to receive the prayers of those two pilgrims thy lips . . .

Marlowe Too far.

Viola I could not sully thy lips gilded with such golden words.

Will Lady, you will burnish them to brighter eloquence. (*To Marlowe.*) Help me up, Kit.

  Will gets on Kit's shoulders.

Viola Good sir, do not use yourself all up.

Will

With love's light wings, did I o'erperch these walls.
For stony limits cannot hold love out,
And what love can do, that dares love attempt.
Therefore thy kinsmen are no stop to me.

Marlowe Very good.

Will Thank you.

*As Will struggles with Marlowe's help to gain a
purchase on the balcony, Viola is distracted by a noise
within.*

Nurse My Lady!

Viola Oh go away!

Nurse Your father comes.

Viola goes in. Will pulls himself up.

Will (*to himself*) I am fortune's fool, I will be punished
for this.

*As Will hauls himself up. The Nurse comes on to the
balcony, sees Will.
She screams. Drums.
Nurse runs inside. Noises within.*

Voices What ho! Lights!

Marlowe Jump!

*Will jumps just in time. Sir Robert appears on the
balcony with a candelabra. Alarums.*

Idiot.

Men run out of the house with flaming lanterns.

Sam Where did they go?

Peter They went that way.

Sam Which way?

Wessex You that way. You this way. Go!

SCENE NINE
FIRST REHEARSALS

Rehearsals, day one.

Fennyman Is this it?

Henslowe Yes.

Fennyman Is this a rehearsal?

Henslowe Yes.

Fennyman Is it always like this?

Henslowe Yes.

Fennyman Is it going well?

Henslowe Very well.

Fennyman But nothing seems to be happening.

Henslowe Exactly. But it's all happening very well.

Fennyman Who is that?

Henslowe Nobody. The author.

Fennyman If this doesn't work, Henslowe, you are forcemeat.

Henslowe calls Shakespeare over.

Henslowe Will, Will! It starts well, but then it gets all long-faced. Where's the comedy, Will? Where's the dog? Do you think it's funny?

Ralph (*looking at the new script*) I was a Pirate King, now I'm a Nurse. That's funny.

Henslowe We are at least four acts short, Will.

33

Will We are short of any discernible acting talent, those that we have are over-parted ranters and stutterers who should be sent back to the stocks. Let's wait for Ned Alleyn. We can't even be sure we have a Romeo. Who are you?

Webster I'm Ethel, sir, the pirate's daughter.

Will I'm damned if he is!

He boots Webster up the backside.

Henslowe I think he has potential.

Will This is a shambles.

Henslowe I think we should get started.

Will Gentlemen! Good men all.

Henslowe (*to Fennyman*) It is customary to make a little speech on the first day. It does no harm and the authors like it.

Will Firstly, gentlemen, I want to thank you all for coming here today. I am honoured to be working with such an extraordinary calibre of actor. Today we are about to embark on a mysterious journey, a journey which . . .

Fennyman I'll speak the speech.

Will I haven't quite finished.

Fennyman Shut it! Now you listen to me, you dregs! Actors are ten a penny and I, Hugh Fennyman, hold your nuts in my hand so –

Noise from offstage. Suddenly a group of men enter headed by Ned Alleyn, the actor – a handsome piratical figure with a big voice and big sword.

Ned Huzzah! I am returned!

Fennyman Excuse me, I was speaking the speech.

Ned Silence, you dog. I hear there is a play for me.

Fennyman Who are you, sir?

Ned Who am I? I am Hieronimo! I am Tamburlaine!
I am Faustus! I am Barabas the Jew – oh yes, Master
Will, and I was Henry the Sixth several times. Who are
you, sir?

Fennyman I am the money.

Ned Then you may remain, as long as you remain silent.
Congratulations, sir. Your investment is safe in the hands
of Ned Alleyn. What is the play? What is my part?

Will We are in desperate want of a Mercutio, Ned, a
young nobleman of Verona.

Ned (*unimpressed with the location*) Verona, again. And
what is the title?

Will *Mercutio.*

Ned I will play him! Divide the rest betwixt the boys
and watch how genius creates a legend.

Will Mr Pope! Mr Phillips! Mr Hemmings! Mr Condell!
Mr Tooley! Mr Wabash! Mr Nol! Sam, my pretty one!
Are you ready to fall in love again?

Sam I am, Master Shakespeare.

Will But your voice . . . have they dropped?

Sam No, no, a touch of cold.

Fennyman Actually, Master Shakespeare, I saw his
Tamburlaine. Wonderful.

Will Yes, I saw it.

Fennyman Of course, it was mighty writing. There is no
one quite like Marlowe.

Will No indeed. Master Henslowe, you have your actors.
Except Thomas Kent.

He sees Webster is still there.

Are you still here, boy?

Webster I was in one of your plays before. They cut my head off in *Titus Andronicus*. When I write plays they will be like *Titus*.

Will You admire it.

Webster No. But I like it when they cut heads off. And the daughter mutilated with knives. Plenty of blood. That's the only writing.

Ned, now with pages, stops Will.

Ned Will . . . where is Mercutio?

Will I am saving my best for him. I leave the scene in your safe-keeping, Ned. Cut round what's his name, Romeo, for now.

Ned Who?

Will Nobody. Mercutio's friend.

He turns to find Kent.

Master Kent! I almost didn't recognise you.

Henslowe Places, please.

Ned Gather around, gentlemen.

Then unexpectedly Burbage arrives.

Burbage Shakespeare! You cur. I thought I would find you here. Where's Ethel?

Will Who?

Burbage The pirate's daughter I paid two sovereigns for. Mr Alleyn.

Ned Mr Burbage.

Burbage The Prince of the Provinces. Where is my play, Shakespeare? I have postered half of Shoreditch and I haven't seen a single page.

Will They're coming, they're coming.

Burbage If you've sold my play to Henslowe I'll slice you nape to chops.

He stops Ned.

What play is this, Alleyn?

Ned *Mercutio.*

Henslowe Out of this theatre, you overripe ham. We are trying to rehearse. Gentlemen. Romeo laments his Ethel.

Now Kent and Nol (as Benvolio) rehearse, their parts in hand.

Will May I, Mr Alleyn?

Ned nods.

Master Kent is playing Romeo, and Master Nol is Benvolio. Gentlemen, a scene in Verona.

Viola/Kent
Ay me, sad hours seem long.
Was that my father that went hence so fast?

Nol
It was. What sadness lengthens Romeo's hours?

Viola/Kent
Not having that which, having, makes them short.

Henslowe He's good.

Nol
In love?

Viola/Kent
Out.

Nol (*completely over-acting*)
Of love?

Viola/Kent
Out of her favour where I am in love.

Shakespeare interrupts.

Will No no, may I? Don't spend it all at once!

The rehearsal stops as Will gets up.

He is speaking about a baggage we never even meet!
What will be left in your purse when he meets his Juliet?
What will you do in Act Two when he meets the love of
his life?

Viola/Kent I am very sorry, sir, I have not seen Act Two.

Will Of course. It is not yet written. At a ball – Sam,
will you come down – he sees the most beautiful girl in
Verona. All thoughts of Ethel. All thoughts of anything
are wiped from his mind and he can think of only her.
At the ball they meet, they share a moment but are torn
asunder. That night he steals to her balcony. And in the
darkness he looks to the window, he sees a torch and
woos her with a transport of poetry – 'But soft, what
light through yonder window breaks? It is the east and
Juliet is the sun.'

Sam It's beautiful.

Will 'Arise fair sun . . .'

Henslowe (*interrupting*) What about Ethel? I paid for a
pirate's daughter.

Will Patience. All will come together.

Viola/Kent Does Romeo get his Juliet?

Will Of course. It is a comedy.

38

Fennyman Enough 'speaky speaky'. Let's get on with it.

Henslowe From the top.

Ned Gentlemen. Capulets stage left, Montagues stage right. And square up.

As everyone sets their positions, Will steals a private word with Kent.

Will Thomas, Master Kent, I have a letter for Lady Viola de Lesseps. The lady of your house. You know her?

He has a letter.

Viola/Kent As well as I know myself, sir. What is it about?

Will Fourteen lines. Give it to her. I shall ever be in your debt.

Everybody peels off, leaving Viola alone on stage. She reads the letter. Music.

SCENE TEN
LORD WESSEX ARRIVES TO MEET VIOLA

Viola (*reading the letter*) Oh, it is complete.

The company onstage hold their positions.

Shall I compare thee to a summer's day?
Thou art more lovely and more temperate
Rough winds do shake the darling buds of May
And summer's lease hath all too short a date.

Sometime too hot the eye of heaven shines
And often is his gold complexion dimm'd
And every fair from fair some time declines
By chance or nature's changing course untrimm'd.
But thy eternal summer shall not fade
Nor lose possession of that fair thou owest.

Nor shall death brag thou wander'st in his shade
When in eternal lines to time thou growest.
So long as men can breathe or eyes can see
So long lives this and this gives life to thee.

Oh I am made immortal!

*Music. There is a flurry of movement and sound as
the held company break and move to observe the next
scene. The Nurse runs on.*

Nurse My Lady. My Lady. My Lady. Where have you
been? Lord Wessex demands to come in. He's waiting
downstairs. Quickly, you must change.

*Viola runs off to get changed. Wessex paces on the
balcony.*

Viola (*off, as she changes*) How long has he been here?

Nurse All morning.

Viola (*off*) What did you tell him?

Nurse I told him you were at prayer, My Lady.

Viola (*off*) For four hours?

Nurse I said you were pious, My Lady.

Viola (*off*) Why is he here today?

Nurse You know perfectly well, My Lady.

Wessex Nurse, Nurse, where is the future Lady Wessex?

Nurse You must have patience, sir. My lady is still in the
act of contemplation.

Wessex Lengthy orisons for one so young.

Nurse She always was a pious little girl, My Lord. My
mistress is the sweetest lady, My Lord and still as pious.
Lord, Lord, even when she was a prating child, sir, she

would spend hours on her knees. I used to swear she'd wear them out!

Wessex Oh for heaven's sake, where the devil is she?!

Nurse My Lady, My Lady, Lord Wessex is here.

Viola returns, immaculately dressed, in the nick of time.

Wessex My Lady.

Viola Lord Wessex. You have been waiting.

Wessex I am aware of it. It is beauty's privilege. Though four hours' prayer is less piety than self-importance. I have spoken to the Queen. Her Majesty's consent is requisite when a Wessex takes a wife, and once gained her consent is her command.

Viola Do you intend to marry, My Lord?

Wessex Your father should keep you better informed. He has bought me for you. He returns from his estates to see us married two weeks from Saturday. You are allowed to show your pleasure.

Viola But I do not love you, My Lord.

Wessex How your mind hops about! Your father was a shopkeeper, your children will bear arms and I will recover my fortune. That is the only matter under discussion today. You will like Virginia.

Viola Virginia?

Wessex Why yes! My fortune lies in my plantations. The tobacco weed. I need four thousand pounds to fit out a ship and put my investments to work. I fancy tobacco has a future. We will not stay there long, three or four years.

Viola But why me?

Wessex It was your eyes. No, your lips.

He kisses her with more passion than ceremony. Viola slaps him.

Will you defy your father and your Queen?

Viola The Queen has consented?

Wessex She wants to inspect you. At Greenwich, come Sunday. Be submissive, modest, grateful. And on time.

Wessex leaves. Viola is bereft. The Nurse sees her distress.

Viola My summer's lease is all too brief. Bring me pen and ink. I must write to William Shakespeare.

Nurse Yes, My Lady.

Music. Will rushes on excitedly with pages . . .

SCENE ELEVEN
SECOND REHEARSALS

Will Gentlemen. New pages!

We are in rehearsal again. The actors gather to receive their pages. When Will has distributed them, Ned Alleyn calls Will over.

Ned Will, hold. Can I have a word?

Will You do not like the speech?

Ned The speech is excellent. 'Oh then I see Queen Mab hath been with you.' Excellent and a good length. But then he disappears for the length of a Bible.

Will But then you have his duel, a skirmish of words and swords such as I never wrote, nor any man. He dies with such a passion and poetry as you ever read – 'A plague on both your houses!'

Ned He dies?!

Henslowe There doesn't appear to be a dog of any kind?

Will There was never going to be a dog.

Henslowe I've just bought it from Will Kemp for three sovereigns. And it's eating me out of house and home.

Will I will try to work it in.

Fennyman I can't wait to find out what happens next. Author, please.

Will The Friar marries the lovers in secret, then Ned, playing Mercutio, gets into a fight with one of the Capulets called Tybalt. Romeo – (*Sees Webster.*) In your dreams – tries to stop them, he gets in Ned's way, I mean Mercutio's way, so Tybalt slays Mercutio and then Romeo slays Tybalt.

Fennyman Wonderful!

He didn't really mean to say that but couldn't help himself. He is embarrassed. Will continues.

Will Then the Prince banishes Romeo from Verona.

Henslowe And that's when he goes on the voyage and gets shipwrecked on the island of the Pirate King. Who has a dog!

Fennyman Enough!

He breaks into high dudgeon.

Cease your prattling. This is not just entertainment. This is art.

Henslowe But I paid Will Kemp three sovereigns for that cruel-hearted cur.

Fennyman Shut it. And then . . . ?

Will And then . . . it all works out in the end.

Fennyman Masterful.

Viola/Kent comes in flustered and late.

Henslowe Ah, Master Kent. You've kindly decided to join us.

Viola/Kent Sorry, there was a terrible snarl-up under Putney Bridge.

Fennyman Right. Now you're here let's get on with it.

As the actors take their positions, Ned calls Will over.

Ned Will . . .

Will I know, I know.

Ned It's good.

Will Oh.

Ned But the title. *Romeo and Juliet.* Just a suggestion.

Will Thank you, Ned. You are a gentleman.

Ned And you are a Warwickshire shithouse. The Capulet ball. The dancing begins.

Fennyman Places, please.

The actors dance. Ned directs the scene.

Ned Gentlemen, keep time, distance, proportion. Ready. And. Double forward. And double back. Turn, face your partner. Double away . . . The lovers touch hands . . . That's good . . .

Alleyn is giving shorthand directions as the cast practise the dance.

Ned Next figure. Leaving the lovers.

Viola/Romeo

If I profane with my unworthiest hand
This holy shrine, the gentle sin is this:
My lips, two blushing pilgrims, ready stand
To smooth that rough touch with a tender kiss.

Sam/Juliet

Good pilgrim, you do wrong your hand too much
Which mannerly devotion shows in this
For saints have hands that pilgrims' hands do touch,
And palm to palm is holy palmers' kiss.

*Will, enchanted by Viola's performance, comes closer
to the action. Viola gets distracted.*

Viola/Romeo

Have not saints lips and holy palmers too?

Sam/Juliet

Ay, pilgrim, lips that they must use in prayer.

Viola/Romeo

Oh then, dear saint, let lips do what hands do.
They pray: grant thou, lest faith turn to despair.

Sam/Juliet

Saints do not move though grant for prayers' sake.

Viola is distracted by Will.

It's your cue.

Viola/Romeo

Then move not while my prayer's effect I take.

Viola kisses Sam demurely.

Will Stop! What was that? Sorry, Mr Alleyn.

Ned Carry on, Mr Shakespeare.

Will Master Kent, you kiss like a child. If there is no sin
there is no trespass. Observe. Sam, what was the line?

Sam 'Then move not while my prayer's effect I take.'

Will 'Then move not while my prayer's effect I take.'

Will kisses Sam.

Will You see? Thank you, Ned. Go back.

Musician Three, four . . .

Sam/Juliet
Saints do not move though grant for prayers' sake.

Viola/Romeo
Then move not while my prayer's effect I take.

Before Viola can kiss Sam, Will stops the action.

Will Where is the danger? You are consorting with your family's mortal enemy.

He fills in Juliet.

Now I am Juliet. Let's carry on with the scene.

Musician Three, four . . .

Viola
Thus from my lips, by thine, my sin is purged.

Will/Juliet
Then have my lips the sin that they have took.

Viola/Romeo
Sin from my lips? O trespass sweetly urg'd.
Give me my sin again.

She hesitates, then kisses Will passionately. Even Will is surprised by her enthusiasm. She does not stop.

Ned (*as they continue to kiss*) Thank you – problem solved.

Will Very good, Master Kent.

Ned Let's skip to the end of the scene. 'Exeunt Capulet, Lady Capulet, Guests, Gentlewomen and Masquers.'

Viola/Kent Will, I've got a letter for you from Viola de Lesseps.

Nurse/Ralph and Sam/Juliet do the scene. Will takes this opportunity to open the letter.

Sam/Juliet
Come hither, Nurse. What is yond gentleman?
Go ask his name. If he be married
My grave is like to be my wedding bed.

Ralph/Nurse
His name is Romeo and a Montague,
The only son of your great enemy.

Will reads the letter and becomes increasingly despondent. We then hear the content of the letter.

Viola William, I am to be married to Lord Wessex a week on Saturday. The place is dangerous – you must not try to see me again. Please do not try to visit me again.

Will, deeply upset, screws up the letter, and puts it in his pocket.

Peter Juliet! Juliet!

Viola runs off.

Ned No, no, no. Too early. He's not finished yet. Are you all right, Will? Carry on.

Sam/Juliet
Of one I danc'd withal.

Ralph/Nurse
Anon, anon!
Come, let's away, the strangers all are gone.

Will (*upset by the letter*) Purgatory, torture, hell itself.

Ralph/Nurse I wasn't that bad.

Will Master Kent!

Scene change.

SCENE TWELVE
THE BOAT SCENE

Viola in the boat. Members of the company create noises of the river and the boat.

Viola/Kent Boatman. Down river. De Lesseps Hall, please. On the double.

The boat is about to pull away when Will comes running.

Will Thomas!

He catches the boat up and leaps on board.

Boatman Steady on, guvnor.

Viola/Kent Will!

Will I have to speak with you.

Boatman Hang on a minute. I know your face. You're an actor. I saw you in something.

Will Very possibly.

Boatman What was it? The one with a king.

Viola/Kent Please, I'm in a hurry.

Boatman I had that Christopher Marlowe in the back of my boat once.

The Boatman pulls away.

Will Oh Thomas, I am undone, my strings are cut – I'm a puppet in a box.

Boatman Writer as well, are you?

Will Row your boat!

He pulls out the letter.

She tells me to keep away. She is to marry Lord Wessex.

Viola/Kent If you love her you must do as she asks.

Will And break her heart and mine?

Viola/Kent It's only yours you can know.

Will She loves me, Thomas!

Viola/Kent Does she say so?

Will No.

He changes position in the boat, sitting very close to Viola.

And yet she does where the ink has run with tears. Was she weeping when she gave you this?

Viola/Kent I . . . her letter came to me by the nurse.

Will Your aunt?

Viola/Kent Yes, my aunt. Perhaps she wept a little. Tell me how you love her, Will.

Will Like a sickness and its cure together.

Viola/Kent Yes, like rain and sun, like cold and heat. (*Collecting herself.*) Is your lady beautiful? Since I came to visit from the country, I have not seen her close. Tell me, is she beautiful?

Will Oh, Thomas, if I could write the beauty of her eyes! I was born to look in them and know myself.

Viola/Kent And her lips?

Will Oh, Thomas, her lips! The early morning rose would wither on the branch, if it could feel envy!

Viola/Kent And her voice? Like lark song?

Will Deeper, softer. None of your twittering larks! I would banish nightingales from her garden before they interrupt her song.

Viola/Kent She sings too.

Will Constantly. Without doubt. And plays the lute, she has a natural ear. And her bosom, Thomas. Thomas, did I mention her bosom?

Viola/Kent What of her bosom?

Will Oh, Thomas, a pair of pippins! As round and rare as golden apples.

Viola/Kent I think the lady is wise to keep your love at a distance. For what lady could live up to it close to, when her eyes and lips and voice may be no more beautiful than mine? Besides, can a lady born to wealth and noble marriage love happily with a Bankside poet and player?

Will Yes, by God! Love knows nothing of rank or riverbank! It will spark between a queen and the poor vagabond who plays the king, and their love should be minded by each, for love denied blights the soul we owe to God! So tell My Lady, William Shakespeare waits for her in the garden.

Viola/Kent But what of Lord Wessex?

Will For one kiss I would defy a thousand Wessexes!

Viola is overcome. She kisses him.

Viola/Kent Oh Will.

Will is amazed. Viola runs off throwing money at the Boatman.

Will Wait.

Boatman Thanks, M'Lady.

Will Lady?!

Boatman Viola de Lesseps. Knew her since she was this high. Always a bit of a tomboy. But the facial hair is a big surprise.

Will is in shock.

Boatman Strangely enough I'm a bit of a writer myself.

The Boatman produces a brick-sized manuscript.

It wouldn't take you long to read it. 'Spect you know all the booksellers . . .

When Will is shot of the Boatman he throws the manuscript into the river. Marlowe, one of the observers, gives him a ladder so Will can get into Viola's bedroom.

SCENE THIRTEEN
VIOLA'S SECOND BEDROOM

Viola runs into her bedroom, distraught.

Nurse My Lady?

SONG – 'WHAT IS LOVE?'

Company

> *What is love?*
> *Is love hereafter?*
> *Present mirth is present laughter.*
> *What's to come is still unsure*
> *Youth's a stuff will not endure.*

Viola starts to take off her Kent clothes. She lets her hair down, rips off her doublet so she is now wrapped only in the binding and breeches. Enter Will.

Will Viola? Master Kent?

Shocked by his voice, Viola turns to face him. She still has the Kent moustache.

O brave new world! Are you my actor or my muse?

Viola I am both but should be neither.

Will Can you love a fool?

Viola Can you love a player?

Will If she is a maid.

He takes off her moustache and passes it to the observing Marlowe.

Viola Sir, I am a lady.

They kiss.

Will Wait! You are still a maid and perhaps mistook in me as I was mistook in Thomas Kent.

Viola Are you not the author of the plays of William Shakespeare?

Will I am.

Viola Then kiss me again for I am not mistook.

They kiss again.

You have bound me to you.

Will Then let me unbind thee.

He tries to take her to the bed to unwind her binding but she takes pages from his pocket.

Viola What is this?

Will Nothing.

Viola What are these pages?

Will They can wait.

Viola No, I must see them.

Viola reads. Music gently starts.

But soft, what light through yonder window breaks?
Is it the east and Juliet is the sun.
Arise fair sun and kill the envious moon
Who is already sick and pale with grief
That thou her maid art far more fair than she.

Oh, Will!

Will Do you like it?

*He takes the pages from her and kisses her. She
snatches them back, eager to read on.*

Viola
The brightness of her cheek would shame those stars
As daylight doth a lamp.

You –

She makes Will read Romeo. He knows it by heart.

Will
See how she leans her cheek upon her hand.
Oh that I were a glove upon that hand
That I might touch her cheek.

Viola takes the pages.

Viola
Ay me!

This is wondrous.

Will (*from memory*)
She speaks.
O speak again, bright angel . . .

Viola (*reading*)
Romeo, Romeo, wherefore art thou Romeo?

Will
Oh be some other name.

Viola
What's in a name? That which we call a rose
By any other word would smell as sweet.
Romeo, doff thy name
And for thy name, which is no part of thee
Take all myself.

They kiss.

Viola (*she reads on, doing Will's bits as well*)
I take thee at thy word
Call me but love, and I'll be new baptised.

Sweet Montague, be true,
Stay but a little, I will come again.

Will
O blessed, blessed night. I am afeard,
Being in night, all this is but a dream,
Too flattering sweet to be substantial.

Viola (*alarmed by the stage directions*) She leaves?

Will But returns. I came on something. The friar who marries them will take up their destinies.

Viola So it will end well for love?

Will In heaven perhaps. It is not a comedy I am writing now.

Viola A tragedy?

Will The course of true love ne'er did run smooth. Come, there will be time for plays.

Will kisses Viola, trying to pull her down to the bed, but she resists.

Viola Wait. There is more.

I would I were thy bird.

Sweet, so would I.
Yet I should kill thee with much cherishing.

She flips on to another moment.

My bounty is as boundless as the sea.

Will *and* **Viola**
My love as deep.

Will
The more I give to thee,
The more I have. For both are infinite.

The two lovers are on the bed.
  Music swells.
  Marlowe and another company member slowly converge on the bed and close the curtains.

End of Act One.

Act Two

Gentle music and lights slowly up on a huge four-poster bed. The curtains are still closed. Music.

SONG – SHALL I COMPARE THEE

Musicians
> *Shall I compare thee to a summer's day?*
> *Thou art more lovely and more temperate*
> *Rough winds do shake the darling buds of May*
> *And summer's lease hath all too short a date.*
> *Too short a date.*

As the musicians continue to play instrumentally we become aware of coital noises from within. Viola grows louder and louder until climax.

Viola *(still out of breath)* I would not have thought it. There is something better than a play.

Will There is?

Viola Even your play.

Will Well, perhaps better than *The Two Gentlemen of Verona.*

Viola And that was only my first try.

They open the curtains. They are naked with their modesty preserved by bedclothes.

You would not leave me?

Will I must. Look – how pale the window.

Viola Moonlight.

Will You're right – let Henslowe wait.

Viola Henslowe!?

Will Let him be damned for his pages!

Viola Oh no. No.

Will There is time. It is still dark.

Viola It is broad day. The cockerel tells us so.

Will It was the owl. Believe me, love, it was the owl.

Viola You would leave us players without a scene to read today?

Nurse knocks.

Nurse (*off*) My Lady.

Viola Go away.

> *They shut the bed curtains. Nurse enters with Viola's clothes in a large laundry basket singing 'O Mistress Mine'.*

Nurse

> *O mistress mine, where are you roaming?*
> *O stay and hear your true love's coming.*

My Lady. It is a new day.

> *Nurse comes in. Will creeps out of bed and manages to stand behind her.*

Viola It is a new world.

Nurse My Lady . . . It is Sunday. You are already due at Greenwich, to meet the Queen. (*Singing.*) 'Trip no further, pretty sweeting.'

> *She opens the curtains, sees Will. Pause,*

Nurse (*sentimentally*) Ahhh!

Wessex Where is she? Damn you.

Nurse My Lady, Lord Wessex awaits.

Wessex enters, outside Viola's bedchamber.

Wessex (*to observing company*) Out of my way! (*To Nurse.*) I demand her to be brought to me.

The Nurse leaves Will to help Viola get dressed and goes to Wessex.

Nurse Hold your horses, My Lord. I'm coming as fast as I can. As my mother used to say, patience is a virtue. Be patient, My Lord, she is dressing.

Viola desperately puts clothes on.

Wessex Will you ask Her Majesty to be patient? The Queen Gloria Regina, God's Chosen Vessel, the Radiant One, who shines her light on us, is at Greenwich today, and prepared, during the evening's festivities, to bestow her gracious favour on my choice of wife – and if we're late the old boot will not forgive. So either you produce her with or without her undergarments or I will drag her out myself.

Nurse Of course, My Lord, she won't be long.

Will You cannot marry him! Not for the Queen herself!

Viola thrusts the naked Will into hiding.

Viola What will you have me do? Marry you instead?

Will Yes.

Viola Idiot. It's impossible. I must go to Greenwich today.

Will I will go with you.

Viola Wessex will kill you.

Will I know how to fight.

Viola Stage fighting. Oh Will! As Thomas Kent my heart belongs to you but as Viola the river divides us, and I will marry Wessex a week from Saturday.

Will No. Now that I have found you I will never be parted from you.

Wessex I will wait no longer!

Nurse My Lord, you cannot enter a young lady's bedchamber.

Wessex By heaven, I will drag her down by the Queen's command. Convention be damned, I am going in!

As it becomes clear that Wessex is coming in, Viola, by now almost dressed, bundles Will, his clothes and the large laundry basket into the bed and closes the curtains. She positions herself and puts the finishing touches to her dress as Wessex enters.

Nurse My Lady, Lord Wessex is here.

Wessex Ah! My Lady! Here, in your bedchamber, all alone. What on earth has kept you? We are due in Greenwich in less than an hour. And the Queen waits for no one.

Viola I must look presentable.

Wessex The tide waits for no man but I swear it would wait for you! By my heavens, you look good enough to ravish here and now.

He roughly takes Viola's wrist and pulls her to the bed. She resists.

Viola Lord Wessex!

Wessex I said now!

Viola No!

Wessex Now!

He pulls the curtain open. This reveals Will, who has got himself into a dress and headdress.

Will Beg your pardon, My Lord.

Will drops the laundry basket on to the floor, and proceeds to open the curtains and make the bed.

Wessex Who is this?

He pulls open the curtains to reveal Will in a dress.

Viola My . . . laundry maid.

Will And chaperone. My Lady's country cousin. And we'll be kissing cousins when her purse is open to you.

Wessex Do you have many relatives?

Viola None so dear as Cousin Wilhemina, my Lord.

Will You may call me Miss Wilhemina!

Wessex On a more fortuitous occasion, perhaps. Come, Viola, we must go!

Will (*getting very close to Wessex*) Oh, My Lord, you will not shake me off, she never needed me more, I swear by your breeches you be a handsome gallant, just as she said.

Wessex Viola! Come with me.

Will Wait for me, My Lord.

Music. Fanfares lead us into . . .

SCENE TWO
GREENWICH

The Queen, her attendants and Court assemble. Music underscore.

Wessex Now?

Tilney Now, my Lord.

Wessex The Queen asks for you. Answer well.

60

Tilney escorts Viola through the crowd – this is a formal affair. He leads her to the Queen. Being without Viola, Wessex takes Will by the arm.

There is a man behind this pretence.

Will A man, My Lord?

Wessex I am no fool. There was a poet . . . a theatre poet I heard. Does he come to the house?

Will A poet?

Wessex An insolent penny-a-page rogue, Marlowe. A Christopher Marlowe. Has he been to the house?

Will Marlowe. Oh yes, he be the one. Lovely doublet, shame about the verse.

Wessex The dog!

Tilney presents Viola to the Queen.

Queen What a smile you have, Mr Tilney. Like a brass plate on a coffin.

Tilney Thank you, Your Majesty. The Lady Viola de Lesseps.

Viola Your Highness.

Queen Stand up straight, girl.

Viola straightens. The Queen examines her.

I have seen you. You are the one who comes to all the plays . . . at Whitehall, at Richmond.

Viola Your Majesty.

Queen What do you love so much?

Viola Your Majesty . . . ?

Queen Speak out! I know who I am. Do you love stories of kings and queens? Feats of arms? Or is it courtly love?

Viola I love theatre. To have stories acted for me by a company of fellows is indeed –

Queen They are not acted for you, they are acted for me.

A chorus of obsequious laughter follows from Tilney and the Court. This recurs at each of the Queen's witticisms.

And . . .?

Viola I love poetry above all.

Queen Above Lord Wessex? My Lord, when you cannot find your wife you had better look for her at the playhouse.

Tilney Hardly a place for a young lady of breeding, Your Majesty.

Queen Oh, I am all for the theatre, Mr Tilney. But playwrights teach nothing about love, they make it pretty, they make it comical, or they make it lust. They cannot make it true.

Viola Oh, but they can.

A gasp that Viola would dare contradict the Queen.

Tilney Her Majesty is not in the habit of being contradicted.

Viola I mean . . . Your Majesty, they do not, they have not, but I believe there is one who can.

Horrified, Wessex rushes to intervene.

Wessex Lady Viola is . . . young in the world. Your Majesty is wise in it. Nature and truth are the very enemies of playacting. I'll wager my fortune.

Queen I thought you were here because you had none. Well, will anyone take Lord Wessex up on his wager? Mr Tilney?

Tilney The Lord Chamberlain cannot be seen to gamble, Your Majesty.

Queen Lady Viola, it seems no one will risk this wager.

Will Fifty pounds.

Shock and horror. Queen Elizabeth is the only person amused.

Queen I hear from somewhere fifty pounds. A very worthy sum on a very worthy question. Can a play show us the very truth and nature of love? I bear witness to the wager, and will be the judge of it as occasion arises.

Tilney A conceit of genius, Your Majesty.

He leads a scatter of applause.

Queen I have not seen anything to settle it yet. So. The fireworks will be soothing after the excitements of Lady Viola's audience.

The whole Court turns to look at the fireworks.

(*Intimately to Wessex.*) Have her then, but you are a lordly fool. She has been plucked since I saw her last and not by you. It takes a woman to know it.

Wessex (*aside*) Marlowe. I will kill the wretch.

He turns to watch the fireworks just beginning. There are gasps from the crowd at each explosion.

Will I must away to my pages. I will see you at the theatre.

Viola Please, Will, be careful.

Will Don't worry, no one will recognise me here.

He turns and immediately bumps into Marlowe.

Marlowe Will! Is there something you haven't told me?

Will What are you doing here?

Marlowe I have come incognito.

Will What for?

Marlowe Call it a truant disposition. Don't you have a play to write?

Will Yes, but I have a commission of the heart. Lady Viola –

Marlowe (*interrupting*) Don't get distracted, Will. God has given you one face, and you run around with another, in a dress! Leave deception to those better suited. Go home and finish your play. You could be the best of all of us. Besides, what if you were caught?

Will And what about you, Kit?

Marlowe Don't worry, no one is going to recognise me here.

Burbage enters.

Burbage Marlowe.

Marlowe Burbage.

Will moves to exit.

Burbage Hello, young lady.

Will laughs girlishly as he leaves.

Marlowe What are you doing here, Burbage?

Burbage Actually I have come to give my Faustus for Her Majesty this very evening.

Marlowe Your Faustus? Burbage, you thief. You already owe me twenty pounds. My *Massacre at Paris* is completed, or shall I give the play to Ned Alleyn?

Burbage You have the pages?

Marlowe You have the money?

Burbage Tomorrow.

Marlowe Then tomorrow you have the pages. When I've had what I am owed for your royal *Faustus*.

Burbage Come, what is money to men like us? Besides, if I need a play I have another waiting, a comedy by Shakespeare.

Marlowe *Romeo*? He gave it to Henslowe.

Burbage Never!

Burbage I gave Shakespeare two sovereigns for Romeo!

Marlowe You did. But Henslowe rehearses it as we speak.

Burbage Treachery! Traitor and thief.

Marlowe Well, I am to Deptford. Tomorrow.

Burbage Won't you stay, Kit, for my performance?

Marlowe I refuse to stay and see myself murdered here tonight. Twenty pounds, Burbage. The fee simple! Oh, simple!

Burbage Henslowe is rehearsing my play?

Marlowe With Alleyn. As we speak.

SCENE THREE
THE BIG FIGHT

Ned Gentlemen, from the top of the scene, with words.

The scene assembles; Ned, playing Mercutio, and Nol as Benvolio have swords and are squared up against Robin as Tybalt, Peter as Petruccio and Ralph as another Capulet. They too have swords. Elsewhere Wabash measures Sam for a costume, Webster reads a script in a corner and Henslowe and Fennyman look on.

Nol/Benvolio
By my head, here comes the Capulets.

Ned/Mercutio
By my heel, I care not.

Robin/Tybalt
Follow me close for I will speak to them.
Gentlemen good e'en. A word with one of you.

Ned/Mercutio Are you really going to do it like that?

And but one word with one of us? Couple it with
something, make it a word and a blow.

Enter Viola/Kent as Romeo.

Robin/Tybalt
Well, peace be with you, sir. Here comes my man.
Romeo, thou art a villain.

Viola/Romeo
I do protest I never injured thee
But love thee better than thou canst devise
Till thou shalt know the reason of my love
And so, good Capulet, which name I tender
As dear as my own, be satisfied.

Ned/Mercutio
Oh calm, dishonourable, vile submission!
Tybalt, you rat-catcher, will you walk?

Robin/Tybalt
I am for you.

He attacks Ned.

Ned/Mercutio Careful, you're supposed to attack the
shoulder.

Robin has messed up the fight choreography.

Robin/Tybalt
I am for you.

Robin attacks Ned, doing it wrong again.

Ned/Mercutio Shoulder! Wrong shoulder! For God's sake, Peter, show him how it's done. Master Kent, your Romeo.

Ned and Peter fight and Viola and Nol continue to play the scene.

Viola/Romeo
Gentle Mercutio, put thy rapier up.
Draw, Benvolio, beat down their weapons.
Gentlemen, for shame forbear this outrage.
Tybalt, Mercutio. The Prince expressly hath forbid . . .
Hold, Tybalt! Good Mercutio!

Tybalt stabs Mercutio.

Peter/Petruccio Away, Tybalt!

Peter gives his sword to Robin, and Robin continues as Tybalt. He runs off.

Nol/Benvolio
What, art thou hurt?

Ned/Mercutio
Ay, ay, a scratch. Marry 'tis enough.
Ask for me tomorrow and you shall find me a grave man.

Burbage arrives with two in tow and barges through.

Burbage I'll see you hanged, Henslowe! I have come for my play, you scoundrels. Give me that manuscript.

He sees Will with the manuscript, draws his rapier on him and the other two advance.

Ned How dare you. sir? No one interrupts my rehearsals.

Burbage *Your* rehearsals?

Ned Ignore him, Master Kent – continue!

Burbage Give me that manuscript.

Will throws his inkwell at Burbage as Burbage and his men lunge for him. Will sprints to avoid them.

Viola Quick, Will. Careful, Will, don't let him get it.

Will (*throwing the manuscript to Henslowe*) Henslowe, catch!

Ned Out of my rehearsals, you talentless dog. I will chop you to pieces.

Burbage Upstairs. Get that manuscript.

Ned Henslowe. Do something . . .

Henslowe I am doing something.

Ned Out, vile jelly!

Sam Down here. Down here.

Burbage Stop him. Get it!

Henslowe Catch it, Master Kent.

Henslowe throws the manuscript down towards Viola. It is exactly where Webster is standing, reading his script. Both Viola and Webster reach up to catch it, and in that split second Viola ends up with the script Webster was reading. Webster, unalarmed, continues to read, now reading Romeo and Juliet.

Burbage I'll not leave here till I have it.

Henslowe How dare you barge in here, you overripe pudding.

Ned I've had enough of you, you ridiculous cur.

Burbage Give me that manuscript!

Ned I will chop your spine off!

Ned and Burbage go into a full-scale sword fight, while the swapped manuscript is being fought over all around the stage.

Will Master Kent, the manuscript. Master Kent.

Henslowe Why don't you leave off fighting till you're Tamburlaine, Burbage?

Burbage Heavy I'm going to rip your throat out, Shakespeare. Give it here.

In the tussle, Burbage's Heavy slams Will and Nol's heads together and gets the swapped manuscript. Burbage has incapacitated Ned, who is lying at his sword-point.

(*Giving Burbage the swapped manuscript.*) Mr Burbage.

Burbage Your swordplay's a little rusty, Alleyn. (*Believing the script he holds to be* Romeo and Juliet.) Thank you, Master Shakespeare. The play's the thing! Rehearsals will begin with me, Monday at the Curtain.

Burbage and his men leave.

Henslowe Let's not panic, we'll think of something.

Fennyman You're an idiot. I was just starting to enjoy myself. Henslowe, there's the small matter of sixteen pounds, five shillings and ninepence . . .

Webster (*reading from the manuscript*) 'That which we call a rose by any other name would smell as sweet.'

Henslowe What's that?

Webster Juliet.

Will snatches the manuscript and pushes Webster to one side.

Will This is my play.

Webster Yeah. I was learning that.

Viola You swapped it?

Webster Yeah, I swapped it for *Gammer Gurton's Needle*.

Will Master Henslowe, the manuscript.

Henslowe We are saved!

Fennyman Gentlemen. A famous victory! We have the manuscript. (*Cheers.*) A cause for celebration.

Cheers. Company hold, except for Will and Viola. Musical tone.

Will Viola. Are you all right?

Viola/Kent Oh, Will. I have never been happier.

Will Come, let's get you dressed.

Viola/Kent No, I want to have a drink with the lads.

Will I really don't think that's a good idea.

Viola/Kent And then I'm gonna drink you under the table.

They kiss passionately. From out of the frozen company crawls Webster. He moves around the kissing couple, observing.

SCENE FOUR
THE BROTHEL/TAVERN

Fennyman Gentleman, actors, swordsmen. You are welcome. The kegs and legs, open and on me.

The company release their hold and set up the brothel. Music and jigging.

(*To Musicians.*) Shut it. (*To everyone.*) Everything, and I mean everything, is on me.

They all cheer.

Molly Brace yourselves, girls.

Fennyman Sam. I think it is time you sampled the delights of a real, living, breathing lady.

Cheers. Sam is hoisted on to someone's shoulder. His bottom is slapped by the assembled crew – a ritual. He is taken to Molly and the two go off to do the deed.

Off you go.

Viola looks around amazed.

Viola/Kent I thought this was a tavern.

Will It is also a tavern.

Viola/Kent This is a house of ill repute.

Will But of good reputation. Come there's no harm in drink.

Kate, a younger girl, straddles Will.

Kate I remember you! The poet.

Will is horrified.

Will Must have been someone else. Thomas Dekker, perchance?

Kate No, I remember you have a silver tongue.

Viola pulls Kate round.

Viola/Kent Excuse me. We're trying to have a conversation.

Kate Now here's a pretty one!

Kate takes an interest in Viola/Kent.

Viola/Kent Excuse me, darling, I'm trying to have a drink.

She tries to get rid of Kate.

Fennyman Master Kent! Will you not dip your wick, sir?

Viola/Kent My wick?

Viola is hoisted on someone's shoulder – it is the ritual as before.

Fennyman All paid for.

Viola wriggles off on to the floor and Will comes to her rescue by diverting everyone's attention.

Will Master Fennyman! Master Fennyman! Master Fennyman, we were in fact discussing your great love of the theatre and Master Kent suggested you should have a part in the play.

Fennyman Me?!

Will I am writing an Apothecary, a small but vital role.

Fennyman By heaven I thank you. I will play . . . No, no, I will be your Apothecary.

I am to be in the play!

Kate What's this play about then?

Ralph Well, there's this nurse . . .

Nol Oi, oi! He's back.

Sam suddenly reappears, a huge smile on his face. There is a huge cheer.

Sam It was very quick.

Molly It was *very* quick.

Sam But I liked it.

Fennyman Come, Sam, take some ale. (*To Henslowe.*) Mr Henslowe, Mr Shakespeare has given me the part of the Apothecary.

Henslowe The Apothecary? What about the shipwreck? How does it end, Will?

Will By God, I wish I knew.

Henslowe I paid for pirates, clowns and a happy end. If I don't get reconciliations and a jig I will send you back to Stratford . . . To your wife!

That goes down very well with the entire company, apart from Viola and Will.

Viola/Kent Wife?!

Will Erm . . .

Henslowe And the twins!

The company hold except for Will and Viola. Musical tone.

Will (*to Viola*) I can explain.

Viola rushes to the door. Will follows.

I was only eighteen. My marriage is long dead and buried in Stratford. Everything I am is here in London. With you.

Viola/Kent I have risked everything and you have served me with lies. I will never see you again.

Viola tries to leave, Will gets in her way.

Will No.

Viola avoids his touch.

I love you.

I love you more than all writing.

I love you more than life itself.

Viola runs out, evading Will as Peter runs in.

Peter Will! Mr Henslowe! Gentlemen all! A black day for us all! There is news come up river from Deptford.

Marlowe is dead. Stabbed! Stabbed to death in a tavern in Deptford. Kit Marlowe is dead.

Will is horror-stricken.

Will What have I done?

Ned He was the first man among us.

Music starts.

A great light has gone out.

The company slowly dismantle the brothel and set up the next scene while watching Will.

Will Kit. Kit . . .

SONG – 'BUT THY ETERNAL SUMMER'

But thy eternal summer shall not fade
Nor lose possession of,
Nor lose that fair thou ow'st,
Nor shall death, brag thou wander'st
   in his shade.

Viola is brought on in the bed, sobbing.

SCENE FIVE
CAVEAT EMPTOR

Nurse meets Viola on the bridge.

Nurse My Lady.

Will Wessex.

Will runs off.

Nurse My Lady, My Lady, what's the matter?

Viola Leave me, Nursey.

Viola gets off the bridge followed by the Nurse. She rips off her 'Kent' disguise in a tearful rage, fierce with grief.

Wessex Viola!

Nurse Lord Wessex is here.

Viola Tell him I'm asleep, tell him anything, just make him go away.

Wessex bursts in.

Wessex Let me through!

Nurse No! Sir . . .

Nurse I'm sorry, Ma'am.

Wessex stands before her, smouldering with drink-fuelled lust.

Wessex Ah my sad, sweet angel.

Viola What is the meaning of this?!

Wessex Here you are. Ready. Undone. I have been minded, your father away, that as he is paying good money for me that I should at least allow you the privilege of caveat emptor. Buyer beware. One would hate you to be disappointed on the wedding night if you found the purchase not in good working order. (*To Nurse.*) Leave us. A pint of Madeira when I call. (*To Viola.*) I see you have been crying. I understand, of course. I never met the poor fellow but once in your house. But you have my commiserations.

Viola 'Poor fellow'?

Wessex Oh! Dear God, I did not think it would be me to tell you! A great loss to theatre, to playwriting, dancing and so forth.

Viola I don't understand.

75

Wessex Your playwright is dead.

Viola Dead?! Impossible.

Wessex Stabbed to death this very night, in a tavern, I heard.

She faints. Wessex starts to unbutton himself.

Exquisitely sensitive.

A crack of thunder.

Nice weather for it. (*Shouting to Nurse*) Nursey, I'll have that Madeira.

Will Viola!

Wessex (*irritated at the interruption*) Odds fish! Marlowe!

Meanwhile, Will has climbed over the balcony, bedraggled, haunted, otherworldly. He comes into the room. Wessex gasps in horror.

Marlowe!

Will screams:

Will Aaargh!

This terrifies Wessex further.

Wessex Avaunt and quit my sight, thou phantom.

Wessex draws his dagger.

Will No.

Will comes forth with hands up to plead mercy:

Wessex Spare me, for the love of God!

He flees. Will is completely confused, then sees Viola and rushes to her.

Will Oh my love. If there be no breath on your lips let the worms have me too.

He kisses her. She stirs.

Viola He said you were dead?

Will No, I am alive.

Viola You were stabbed in a tavern?

Will No, no, it's worse . . . Marlowe. Unwittingly I led him to his death. I would exchange all my plays to come for all his that will never be, do you understand? Kit is dead, he was the brightest light of us all, he was my friend and I led him to his death. And all of my stuff is just worthless now, just scribblings in the wind.

Will takes out pages and tears them up.

I'll never write again. Oh God, oh God, Kit, Kit.

Viola picks up the pieces of paper.

Viola Oh my darling, this is madness, Marlowe is dead, but you must live. You must write. Would Kit have wanted this?

She pieces the pages together and reads.

Wilt thou be gone? It is not yet near day.
It was the nightingale and not the lark
That pierced the fearful hollow of thine ear.
Nightly she sings on yon pomegranate tree.
Believe me, love, it was the nightingale.

What is this?

Will Nothing, just some new scene I wrote you.

Viola More false words?

Will My love was no lie. It needs no wife from Stratford to tell you I could never marry the daughter of Robert de Lesseps. It is the scene after they have first made love.

From memory:

It was the lark, the herald of the morn,
No nightingale. Look love, what envious streaks
Do lace the severing clouds in yonder east.
Night's candles are burnt out, and jocund day
Stands tiptoe on the misty mountain tops.
I must be gone and live, or stay and die.

Viola

Yond light is not daylight. I know it, I.
It is some meteor that the sun exhales
To be to thee this night a torchbearer.

Will

I have more care to stay than will to go.
Come death, and welcome. Juliet wills it so.

Viola It is beautiful. All my previous passions were
vanity. I did not truly love you till now. And then . . . ?

Will For killing Juliet's kinsman Tybalt, the one who
killed Romeo's friend Mercutio, Romeo is banished from
Verona. But the Friar who married Romeo and Juliet –

*As the speech continues the scene moves from Viola's
room to the Rose theatre.*

SCENE SIX
REHEARSALS AND A SAVIOUR

*As Will speaks, the company gather in costume. Will
gives out the final pages as he explains what the script
contains:*

Will The Friar who married them gives Juliet a potion to
drink. It is a secret potion. It makes her seeming dead.
She is placed in the tomb of the Capulets. She will awake
to life and love when Romeo comes to her side again.

Ralph Excellent.

Will I have not said all. By malign fate, the message goes astray which would tell Romeo of the Friar's plan. He hears only that Juliet is dead. And with this he goes to the Apothecary.

Fennyman That's me.

Will Romeo buys a deadly poison, then enters the tomb to bid farewell to his Juliet who lies cold as stone. He drinks the poison. He dies by her side. Juliet wakes and she sees her Romeo lying there beside her. And so Juliet takes his dagger and with it she kills herself.

Henslowe Well, that will have them rolling in the aisles.

Will It is complete.

Fennyman Sad and wonderful. I have at home a blue velvet cap. I have seen an apothecary with a cap just so. Have I got time to go and get it?

Will I don't think it matters about the cap.

But Fennyman is gone from one exit. Burbage and Wessex arrive at different entrances simultaneously.

Wessex Out of my way. You!

Burbage Shakespeare! You owe me a play.

Wessex Shakespeare?! You are Shakespeare? You inconsequential coward. This time I will cut you to pieces.

Will and Wessex fight. Will grabs a sword from a nearby weapon rack. Will struggles to keep up with Wessex's swordsmanship. Will is disarmed but, as the two crash into the weapon rack, a dagger falls to the ground which Will uses to stab Wessex. Wessex is stunned. Wessex turns to Will and slowly walks to him. Placing his finger on the blade of Will's knife

Wessex pushes it down. It is a retractable theatre dagger. Wessex draws his own, very real, dagger.

This is a dagger.

They continue to fight, with Wessex slashing and stabbing wildly at the unarmed Will. They struggle over the dagger and Will throws Wessex to the ground. Now holding the dagger, Will grabs Wessex's head and brandishes the dagger above him.

Will This is the murderer of Kit Marlowe.

Everyone No!!

Wessex I rejoiced at his death because I thought it was yours. That is all I know of Marlowe.

Ned It is true, Will, it was a tavern brawl. Marlowe attacked, got his own knife in his eye. A quarrel about the bill.

Henslowe The bill! Oh, vanity, vanity.

Ned Not the billing. The bill.

A voice from back surprises them. They all look. It is Tilney with John Webster in tow.

Tilney Enough of this playacting. This theatre is closed.

Henslowe Mr Tilney. What is this?

Tilney The theatre. A pit of sedition, filth and treachery. I'd have them all ploughed into the ground and covered over with lime. Under the seal of the Lord Chamberlain the Rose theatre is closed for public indecency.

Henslowe Admittedly we are under-rehearsed, but is this really a *moral* issue?

Tilney For the displaying of a female on the public stage.

He grabs Sam. He rips off his skirt.

Webster Not him. Her.

Tilney Him?!

Henslowe Master Kent's a woman?!

Webster advances.

Tilney Really?

Webster Look.

Webster whips off her hat and moustache.

Tilney My Lady de Lesseps!

Wessex Viola! Good God. Here. Dressed as a common actor. Tilney, do your duty.

Tilney Henslowe!

Henslowe I'm amazed. I knew nothing of this.

Viola Nobody knew.

Webster He did. I saw him kissing her bubbies.

Tilney Kissing her where?!

Webster In the wardrobe. Him.

Tilney Let me be straight with you. Her Majesty is only too willing to bid these dens of vice farewell. Henslowe, you will never play again. The Rose theatre is closed.

He storms off.

Wessex (*to Will*) I came to have your life. But it is not worth the taking. Viola, come with me.

Viola I am so sorry, Mr Henslowe, Mr Alleyn, Sam, Mr Wabash. I just wanted to be an actor.

Wabash Y-y-y-y-y-you w-w-w-w-were w-w-w-w-wonderful.

Will Take this and remember me.

Wessex Viola!

Viola leaves with Wessex.

Webster Should've let me play Ethel then, shouldn't ya.

Webster exits. Fennyman arrives in his blue cap.

Fennyman Everything all right?

Henslowe Closed before we opened. Let's pack everything up.

Burbage Hold! Enemies. Brothers. Lend me your ears. We may indeed be rivals in art but we are jointly despised as vagrants, tinkers, peddlers of bombast. Which in my case might be true. But (*to Musicians*) gentlemen – (*They start to play.*) My father James Burbage had the first licence to form a company of players and he drew from all the poets of the age. Their fame will be our fame. So let them all know, we are men of parts. We are a fraternity, and we will be a profession. Will Shakespeare has a play. I have a theatre. To be frank the posters are already posted. Damn the Lord Chamberlain. The Curtain is yours.

Henslowe There is no time to be lost. We will play *Romeo* this Saturday at the Curtain.

Burbage But who will be our Romeo?

Will stands utterly bereft.

Henslowe Will. You had better learn the part.

The stage clears except for Will, who stands shattered. Then magisterial music plays.

SCENE SEVEN
THE WEDDING

The Wedding of Wessex and Viola as a dumbshow masque. It is given to beautiful music. Viola appears in a wedding dress. Sir Robert takes her by the hand and leads the bride to Wessex. *The Nurse looks on. The marriage takes place in a grand scene of ceremony all in the language of the theatre of the Court, the language of Inigo Jones – aristocratic theatre contrasting hugely with the speed and fluency of Shakespeare's rough world of the playhouse. Viola is solemn, brokenhearted. The whole scene is formal and excruciating, as we know Viola is consigning herself to a lifetime of misery. The bride and groom are married and finally kiss in a shaft of white light. The scene changes to:*

SCENE EIGHT
ESCAPE

A room in the de Lesseps household. Sir Robert is at a desk, Wessex is in attendance. The Nurse looks on.

Sir Robert de Lesseps Lord Wessex. Son-in-law. I trust you are all set.

Wessex Indeed, sir, we are for Virginia this afternoon. All is as planned. Except for the matter of the money.

Sir Robert de Lesseps By these drafts in my hand you gain five thousand pounds.

Wessex Thank you, but would you oblige me fifty or so in gold? To settle my accounts at the dockside.

He shouts off to Viola.

Come, Viola. We must away.

Sir Robert opens the desk and unlocks the gold.

What is she doing?

Wessex attempts to go upstairs but the Nurse stops him.

83

Nurse Please, sir, may I ask of you that you be good to her, sir?

Wessex Of course.

Nurse Treat her kindly, sir.

Wessex I will.

Nurse You are a good man, sir.

Wessex Thank you.

Nurse I feel it in my heart. A very good man, sir.

Wessex Please let go of my arm. There's a good nursey.

Nurse God bless you, sir.

Wessex extracts himself from the Nurse.

And another thing, sir.

Wessex Let it wait, woman, we must away. Come, Viola. The tide waits for no man.

He goes upstairs and sees that Viola is not there.

Wessex Viola. She's gone!

The Nurse opens up a playbill she has had hidden.

Nurse Gone, sir?

Sir Robert de Lesseps Gone?

Nurse (*aside*) Oh yes, she has gone.

Sir Robert de Lesseps Gone where?

Nurse I don't know, sir.

Wessex, arriving back downstairs, sees the playbill behind the Nurse's back and takes it from her.

Wessex What is this?

As Wessex reads, Fennyman slowly enters on to the stage accompanied by portentous music

By permission of Mr Burbage
A Hugh Fennyman production
of Mr Henslowe's presentation of
The Admiral's Men in performance of
The Excellent and Lamentable Tragedy of
Romeo and Juliet
Featuring Mr Fennyman as the Apothecary
at the Curtain Theatre.

SCENE NINE
BACKSTAGE AT THE CURTAIN

We are at the Curtain.

Fennyman
Such mortal drugs I have but Mantua's law
Is death to any he that utters them.

(*To Musicians.*) Shut it!

Then him. Then me.

The stage erupts with the company.

Henslowe Beginners to the stage, please. This is your two-minute call.

Ned Good luck, gentlemen. Break a leg!

Henslowe Cheer up, Will. It's a full house. Two thousand people.

Will Are you okay, Sam? The whole thing is hopeless.

Henslowe At least it's stopped raining.

Will Half of the company are sick with the flu. The other half have no idea what their lines are. We'll be lynched, Henslowe.

Henslowe Peace, Will. It will all turn out fine in the end. Beginners to the stage quickly, quickly.

Ah, Mr Wabash. Ready for your big moment.

Wabash T-t-t-t-two h-h-h-households b-both alike in d-d-d-dignity . . .

Will We are lost.

Henslowe No, it will turn out well.

Will How will it turn out well?

Henslowe I don't know. It's a mystery.

Will Good luck, Sam.

Sam makes deep growling sounds.

Sam?!

Henslowe All those expectant faces. Expecting a man with a dog.

Never mind, eh?

Good luck everybody.

Company One, two, three . . . to silence.

Henslowe Off we go.

Will Good luck, Mr Wabash.

Wabash B . . . b . . . break a leg yourself, Will.

Henslowe I think he'll be fine. Music, trumpets! And . . . the Chorus. Mr Wabash, on you go.

Music. The whole perspective flips round and we are now looking at the Curtain's stage from the audience's point of view. We are now in the play.

Wabash T-t-t-t-t-t –

Wabash stops and decides to have another go.

T-t-t-t-t t-t-t-t-t-t-t-twooooo . . .

Will Is this actually happening?

Wabash
 – h-h-households b-both alike in dignity
 In fair Verona where we lay our scene
 From ancient grudge break to new mutiny
 Where civil blood makes civil hands unclean.
 From forth the fatal loins of these two foes
 A pair of star-crossed lovers take their life,
 Whose misadventured piteous overthrows
 Doth with their death bury their parents' strife . . .

Music. We are returned to backstage.

Henslowe It's a mystery, Mr Shakespeare. A mystery.

Wabash collapses, overcome.

Will Wonderful!

Wabash W-w-w-was it any g-g-good?

Henslowe Nol and Adam! On you go.

Romeo and Juliet *begins. It continues simultaneous to much of the following action. There are also scene changes where the company rush back and forth setting the scene, and there is a curtain to separate the acting space from backstage, closed when the scene changes are occurring. The focus for the company is always towards the 'onstage' action and there is a great deal of hushed movement back and forth with props, and actors making entrances and exits.*

Sam makes noise . . .	**Nol/Sampson** Gregory, on my word we'll not carry coals.
Will Sam?	

Sam Shakespeare. My voice!

Will Sam! Do me a speech. Do me a line! A word!

Sam Romeo, Romeo!

Will He can't even say a word. We are lost. Again.

Sam Wherefore art thou Romeo?

Henslowe No one will notice.

Will What will we do?

Henslowe Juliet doesn't come on for twenty pages. Give him cider vinegar and honey.

Peter He's been gargling cider vinegar all day, sir.

Adam/Gregory No, for then we should be colliers.

Sampson A dog of the house of Montague moves me.

Gregory Draw thy tool! Here comes two of their house. I will bite my thumb at them.

Abraham Do you bite your thumb at us, sir?

Gregory No. Do you quarrel, sir?

Abraham Quarrel, sir? No, sir.

Sampson Draw, if you be men. Gregory, remember thy swashing blow.

Mercutio Part, fools! Put up your swords; you know not what you do.

Henslowe Go and rest your voice, boy. It will be all right.

Will How can it possibly be all right?

Peter Will, your cue!

Will goes onstage.

Benvolio Good morrow, cousin.

Will/Romeo Is the day so young?

Burbage Everything all right?

Henslowe We have no Juliet.

Burbage No Juliet?

Henslowe He's lost his voice.

Burbage Lost his voice?

Benvolio But new struck nine.

Henslowe Shhh! Yes but it will all be all right.

Burbage How will it be all right?

Will/Romeo Ay me, sad hours seem long.

Henslowe It's a mystery, something will turn up.

Burbage Does anyone else know the part?

Benvolio What sadness lengthens Romeo's hours?

Company No.

Webster I do.

Will/Romeo Not having that which having makes them short.

Burbage It's a disaster!

Henslowe No women backstage!

Benvolio In love?

Viola It's me.

Henslowe Who are you?

Viola Thomas Kent.

Company Shhh!!

Henslowe What are you doing here?

Viola Since I cannot watch the play, please let me hear it from backstage.

Henslowe There will be no play, we do not have a Juliet.

Viola What happened to Sam?

Henslowe We are lost, his voice has just broken, he can't even get a word out.

Ned We have no choice but to cancel the show.

Fennyman Do you realise how long it's taken me to learn this part?

The company set the next scene, in Juliet's bedchamber.

Will Is this a dream? You have come back to me, Lady de Lesseps.

Will/Romeo Out . . .

Benvolio Of love.

Examine other beauties, your lady's love against some other maid.

Benvolio That I will show you shining at this feast.

Will/Romeo I'll go along, no such sight to be shown, but to rejoice in splendour of my own.

Viola I am married, Will. I am de Lesseps no longer. I sail this afternoon.

Will Without me?!

Viola Will. No. These are our last stolen moments. Do not spoil them.

Will I will never be parted from you.

Peter Will. The curtain!

Will opens the curtain to allow Robin and Ralph onstage to play their scene. Backstage Viola speaks along with the scene.

Viola *and* **Robin/Lady Capulet** (*together*) Nurse, where's my daughter? Call her forth to me.

Viola *and* **Ralph/Nurse** (*together*) Now by my maidenhead at twelve year old I bade her come. What lamb, what ladybird.

Ned This is Sam's entrance.

Viola *and* **Ralph/Nurse** (*together*) God forbid, where's this girl? What, Juliet? What, Juliet?

Burbage He can't go on, we must stop the show.

Henslowe I will go make the announcement.

Viola *and* **Ralph/Nurse** (*together*) What, Juliet?

Viola (*alone*) How now, who calls?

The company all hear Viola say this final line.

Ralph/Nurse Your mother.

Ned Do you know this?

Viola Every word.

Ned On.

Viola I can't go on. It's illegal!

Henslowe We'll be lynched if we put a woman on the stage!

Ralph/Nurse Your mother.

Ned There are two thousand people out there who've paid sixpence a ticket.

Burbage We'll be lynched whatever we do.

Ned On!

Viola No, please, no! I can't possibly.

Ned You'll be marvellous.

Ralph/Nurse Your mother.

Viola is pushed onstage. She runs off, but the cast push her back on.

Viola/Juliet Madam, I am here, what is your will?

Robin/Lady Capulet Thou knowst my daughter's a pretty age.

Ralph/Nurse Faith, I can tell her age to an hour.

Robin/Lady Capulet She's not fourteen. Tell me, daughter Juliet, How stands your disposition to be married?

Viola/Juliet It is an honour that I dream not of.

Ralph/Nurse An honour! Were not I thine only nurse, I would say thou hadst suck'd wisdom from thy teat.

Robin/Lady Capulet Well, think of marriage now; Speak briefly, can you like of Paris' love?

Viola/Juliet I'll look to like, if looking liking move: But no more deep will I endart mine eye Than your consent gives strength to make it fly.

Ralph/Nurse Susan and she – God rest all Christian souls! –

Henslowe A mystery. I told you it would be all right

– were of an age: well, Susan is with God; She was too good for me.

Wabash She is w . . . w . . . w . . . wonderful.

Scene continues onstage.

Tilney By the power given to me by Her Royal Majesty –

Company Shhh!!

Tilney I order you to stop this show.

Henslowe Quiet!

Tilney Not even you, Mr Henslowe, can deny that that is a female on the public stage. Nothing will stop me this time.

Webster opens up a trapdoor which earlier we have seen props come out of. Tilney sees the trap and goes to avoid it, but the company converge around him, lift him into the air and then put him down the trap. Webster shouts down the trap before shutting the door.

Webster That'll teach you – should have paid me!

Wessex enters.

Wessex You artless peasants! That is my wife! You curs.

Company Shhhh!!

Henslowe Oh God!

Wessex I will drag her to the West Indies.

Company Shhh!!

Wessex (*drawing his dagger*) This time I spare no quarter, Mr Shakespeare.

The dog bounds onstage and jumps up on Wessex, pushing him over. Will grabs the dagger and everyone is able to drag Wessex into the trapdoor as well.

Henslowe Put him down with Tilney.

Peter Madam, the guests are come.

This line interrupts the scene upstage wherever they are up to.

Robin/Lady Capulet
We follow thee. Juliet, the county stays.

Ralph/Nurse

Go, girl, seek happy nights to happy days.

Viola, Lady Capulet and the Nurse exit.

Viola I did it, Will. I am a player. I am one of you.

The whole perspective flips round again as the company slowly move offstage. Will and Viola are on stage as Romeo and Juliet. They stare at each other.
For a moment we are unsure whether we are in the play or if this is an intense emotional moment of their leaving each other. Music builds throughout their dialogue . . .

Viola/Juliet

Wilt thou be gone? It is not yet near day.
It was the nightingale, and not the lark,
That pierced the fearful hollow of thine ear.
Nightly she sings on yond pomegranate tree.
Believe me, love, it was the nightingale.

Juliet goes to the balcony.

Will/Romeo

It was the lark, the herald of the morn;
No nightingale. Look, love, what envious streaks
Do lace the severing clouds in yonder East.
Night's candles are burnt out, and jocund day
Stands tiptoe on the misty mountain tops.
I must be gone and live, or stay and die.

Viola/Juliet

Yond light is not daylight; I know it, I.
It is some meteor that the sun exhales
To be to thee this night a torchbearer
And light thee on thy way to Mantua.
Therefore stay yet. Thou needest not be gone.

Will/Romeo

Let me be ta'en, let me be put to death.
I am content, so thou wilt have it so.

Viola/Juliet

O think'st thou we shall ever meet again?

Will/Romeo

I doubt it not, and all these woes shall serve
For sweet discourses in our times to come.

Viola/Juliet

Oh God, I have an ill-divining soul.
Methinks I see thee, now thou art so low,
As one dead in the bottom of the tomb.
Either my eyesight fails, or thou look'st pale.

Will/Romeo

And trust me, love, in my eye so do you.
Dry sorrow drinks our blood. Adieu.

I'll say yon grey is not the morning's eye;
'Tis but the pale reflex of Cynthia's brow.
Nor that is not the lark whose notes do beat
The vaulty heaven so high above our heads.
I have more care to stay than will to go.
Come, death, and welcome! Juliet wills it so.

Henslowe Set the table for the Capulet wedding.

*Again we 'flip' perspectives – we are still in the
moment but are now backstage where Will is waiting
after his exit for Viola to join him.*

Will Come with me.

The rest of the company hold.

We will leave now.

Viola But the play?

Will Forget the play. There is no time.

Viola But where would we go?

Will Anywhere.

Viola And leave London? Perhaps I could be poor, Will, but you could never live without the theatre. You are a dead man without words, and I would be your murderer.

Will No.

Viola If my love means you will write no more, you will break my heart and my murderer be. Maybe our love will last twenty years, till we are old and grey. Your words will be immortal. I cannot be the woman who denies the whole world William Shakespeare.

Will I would not be William Shakespeare for the world if I could be with you.

Viola Will, on this stage I have been free and I will ever thank you for it. I will go to Virginia. To grow old and wise.

Will You will never age for me, nor fade, nor die.

Viola Nor you for me.

They kiss.

Write me well.

The rest of the company break their hold and there is a flurry of movement, the lovers separated by the backstage activity.

Henslowe A hit. A palpable hit.

Ned The tomb for the final act.

As one, the entire company create the stage picture for the final tomb, setting candles, the tomb, positioning Viola and Will . . .

Burbage We may be closed down, but this is a special day for the theatre. You will go down with the very greats. Greene, Kyd, Henry Chettle.

Fennyman (*still practising*) Such mortal drugs I have . . .

Ned Come, My Lady, we have no time to lose. Gentlemen –

Everyone is still.

The final act.

The company exit, leaving Will and Viola. Once more the action flips to the audience's point of view.

Will/Romeo
For here lies Juliet, and her beauty makes
This vault a feasting presence, full of light.
A lightning before death. How can I
Call this a lightning?

As Will speaks, the company are peeping out from the flats at the side of the action, all looking on at the heart-rending scene.

Will/Romeo
O my love, my wife,
Death that hath suck'd the honey of thy breath
Hath had no power yet upon thy beauty,
Thou art not conquer'd. Beauty's ensign yet
Is crimson in thy lips and in thy cheeks,
And Death's pale flag is not advanced there.
Here, here, will I remain
With worms that are thy chambermaids.
Eyes, look your last,
Arms, take your last embrace! And lips, O you
The doors of breath, seal with a righteous kiss.

Will kisses her.

A dateless bargain to engrossing death.
Here's to my love! (*He drinks.*) O true apothecary
Thy drugs are quick. Thus with a kiss I die.

Viola/Juliet
Where is my Lord?
I do remember well where I should be
And there I am. Where is my Romeo?
What's here? A cup clos'd in my true love's hand?
Poison, I see, hath been his timeless end.
O churl. Drunk all, and left no friendly drop
To help me after? I will kiss thy lips.
Haply some poison yet doth hang on them
To make me die with a restorative.

*She kisses him. Now everyone backstage is straining
to watch the scene.*

Thy lips are warm!
Then I'll be brief. O happy dagger.
This is thy sheath. There rust, and let me die.

*She stabs herself and falls. Silence. The tableau of the
dead lovers on the floor.*
   *Then suddenly there is a banging beneath and the
Lord Chamberlain bursts out through the top of the
tomb.*

Tilney In the name of Her Majesty, I arrest you all!

He takes some debris from his head.

Lambert/Page Arrest who?

Tilney Everybody! Burbage's men, Henslowe's men, the
whole of English theatre, everyone of you ne'er-do-wells
who stands in contempt of the authority invested in me
by Her Majesty.

Burbage comes out with the others.

Burbage Contempt? You closed the Rose. What charge do you lay against the Curtain?

Tilney That woman is a woman!

The entire audience and the actors recoil and gasp.

Ned A woman?!

Tilney Yes. So in the name of Her Majesty Queen Elizabeth . . .

Then a voice:

Queen (*off*) Have a care with my name, you'll wear it out.

The Queen comes onstage. She is dressed in a black cloak with a hood. She takes it off and reveals her resplendent costume. Now the whole thing looks like a masque. A formal tableau: the Queen – the deus ex machina – at the centre. She notices Tilney's yellow stockings.

Queen Oh, you are sick of self-love, Lord Chamberlain. The Queen of England does not attend exhibitions of public lewdness, so something is out of joint. Come here, Master Kent. Let me look at you.

Viola comes forward and is about to curtsy when she catches the Queen's eye, an arresting eye, which arrests the curtsy and turns it into a sweeping bow.

Yes, the illusion is remarkable and your error, Tilney, easily forgiven, but I know something of a woman in a man's profession, yes, by God. I do know about that. That is enough from you, Master Kent. If only Lord Wessex were here.

Webster He is, Ma'am.

He gets Wessex from the trap.

Wessex Unhand me, you stockfish. Your Majesty.

Queen There was a wager, I remember . . . as to whether a play can show us the very truth and nature of love. I think you lost your wager today. *(To Webster.)* You are an eager boy. Did you like this play?

Webster I liked it when she stabbed herself.

Queen And your name, young man?

Webster John Webster, Your Majesty.

Queen You will go far.

Webster Cor. Fanks!

The Queen fixes Will with a beady eye.

Queen Master Shakespeare. Next time you come to Greenwich, come as yourself and we will speak some more.

Wessex Your Majesty! How is this to end?

Queen As stories must when love's denied with tears and a journey. Those whom God has joined in marriage, not even I can put asunder. Master Kent, Lord Wessex, as I foretold, has lost his wife at the playhouse – go make your farewell and send her out. It's time to settle accounts. How much was the wager?

Wessex Fifty shillings. Pounds.

Queen Give it to Master Kent. He will see it rightfully home.

Wessex gives the purse to Kent. Viola turns and hands the money to Will.

Viola/Kent I believe this is rightfully yours, Master Shakespeare. I wish you a long and glorious career.

Queen (*to Will*) Master Shakespeare, something more cheerful next time . . . for Twelfth Night perhaps. Tragedy is all very well, sir, now for the music. And next time, please, the man with a dog.

The Queen walks off the stage followed by Wessex and Tilney. The players bow as she goes. Tilney spits at them as he follows.

Tilney I'll be revenged on the whole pack of you.

SONG – 'O MISTRESS MINE'

Company
> O mistress mine, where are you roaming?
> O stay and hear your true love's coming
> That can sing both high and low.
> Trip no further, pretty sweeting,
> Journeys end with lovers meeting.
> Every wiseman's son doth know
> Youth's a stuff will not endure.

During the song the company assemble. Viola is revealed on the platform – it is now the deck of her ship. The company raise their arms in a solemn farewell. The platform carrying Viola slowly moves up. Viola looks out as she disappears. The company move back, revealing Will's desk, and gather round it, much as at the beginning of the play. Will sits and starts to write. At first haltingly, then with more and more conviction till he is interrupted, as in the first scene, by Marlowe.

Marlowe Nice one, Will.

Will Angels and ministers of grace defend us. Are you a ghost?

Marlowe If I am not, I'll break my quill. God, you're good.

Will They said you were dead.

Marlowe Yes, they say that. Your health, Will.

Will And yours, Kit.

Marlowe What is next?

Will A new play. For Twelfth Night.

Marlowe Good title.

Will Really?

Marlowe And the comedy?

Will Comedy! What will my hero be but the saddest wretch in the kingdom, sick with lovr?

Marlowe Good start. Let him be . . . a duke.

Will Orsino.

Marlowe Good name. And your heroine?

Will Sold in marriage and halfway to America! And so my story begins at sea . . . a perilous voyage to an unknown land . . . a shipwreck –

Marlowe A shipwreck is good.

Will The wild waters roar and heave . . . the brave vessel is dashed all to pieces and all the hapless souls are drowned –

Marlowe A comedy?

Will – save one. A woman whose soul is greater than the ocean and her spirit stronger than the sea's embrace. Not for her a watery end but a new life beginning on a stranger shore, the province of the duke, Orsino.

Marlowe And then –

Will Fearful of her virtue she comes to him dressed as a boy.

Marlowe Thus unable to declare her love. Funny.

Will No, the comedy is with the clapped-out veterans and cross-gartered prigs who rule the household. Viola is the spirit of freedom, of true love trying against all bounds to be out.

Marlowe But how will it end?

Will Happily.

Marlowe But how?

Will I don't know. It's a mystery.

The candle on Will's desk is blown out by the company. Darkness. The company take the applause and join in a danse generale.